Emerging Trends in Indo-Latin American Relations

Emerging Trends in Indo-Latin American Relations

Edited by
V. Shivkumar

Commonwealth

Emerging Trends in Indo-Latin American Relations

1st Edition : 2002
ISBN 81-7169-692-9

Published by :
Ajay Verma
For Commonwealth Publishers
4831/24, Prahlad Street,
Ansari Road, Darya Ganj,
New Delhi - 110002
Phone : 3272541, 3257835
Fax: 91-011-3257835

Laser Typesetting by:
Stylish Laser Typesetter
Delhi

Printed at:
Roshan Offset Printers
Delhi

Raj Bhavan
Dona Paula
Goa-403004

25 February 1997

P. C. Alexander

Governor of Goa

Message

I am happy to know that the Seminar on Emerging Trends on Indo-Latin American and Caribbean Relations is being held in Goa on 20 and 21 March 1997. I complement the Centre for Latin American Studies, Goa University in taking the initiative to organise this Seminar. I am glad to note that several diplomats from Latin America and Caribbean countries, academicians and scholars will be participating in the Seminar.

It is a matter of great satisfaction that there is growing awareness among the people of India and the Latin American and Caribbean countries about the need for greater cooperation in the fields of culture, trade and industry. I have no doubt that seminars like this will help in further strengthening the relations between India and the Latin American region.

I was invited to address this Conference, but because of my other preoccupations in Mumbai, I am unable to be in Goa on the dates when the Seminar is being held. I take this opportunity to convey my best wishes to all the distinguished participants of this Seminar.

I wish the Seminar every success.

(P.C. Alexander)
Governor of Goa

Preface

The papers presented in this edited volume purports to provide an overview on the emerging trends in Indo-Latin American relations. The first encounter between the leaders of India and Latin America dates back to 1927. The occasion was the meeting of the International Congress against Imperialism held in Brussels. Even after that, the distance and the language have been repeatedly cited as formidable barriers to forge an understanding between the two regions. Influence of Guru Dev Rabindranath Tagore and the political teachings of Mahatma Gandhi and M.N. Roy nevertheless became familiar to the Spanish and Portuguese speaking people of Latin America. The emigration of Indian indentured labourers to Trinidad and Tobago, Jamaica, Guyana and Surinam had further brought an understanding of India's values and culture in these regions. With the active role of India in the Non-Aligned Movement and the Afro-Asian Solidarity in the post-independence era, made India to distance itself from the Western hemisphere nations.

It was only after India's prime minister, Indira Gandhi visited the region in the late 1960s, along with the increasing interaction of the Latin American countries in international affairs, the region assumed considerable importance to India's policy makers. In fairness, it may, however, be mentioned that at least some of the Latin American countries did support India's position on the Kashmir issue at a time when these countries were apparently identified as being part of the Western bloc. Admittedly, Cold War compulsions constrained India to forge close to the Latin American countries. No wonder, the end of the Cold War, created a political ambience which helped promote understanding between India and Latin America facilitating increasing cooperation in areas of trade, joint economic ventures and science and technology.

It is against these encouraging developments, the Centre for Latin American Studies at Goa University thought it fit to organize a conference to study the emerging trends in India-Latin America-Caribbean relations. With this in view, the Centre hosted a two-day conference in 1997 with financial assistance from the Ministry of External Affairs, Government of India. The Conference brought together leading representatives from the Latin American and Caribbean diplomatic corps, academic community, business, government and scientific organizations who engaged themselves in a two-day brain-storming discussion. Late Shri S.P.Godrej, Chairman, Godrej & Boyce Co. gave the valedictory address.

We do hope this volume will provide some insights into Latin America as a region and generate further research and studies regarding India and its multi-faceted relations with Latin America and the Caribbean.

The Editor would like to record his thanks to the University Grants Commission for funding the Latin American Area Studies programme at Goa University. General S. F. Rodrigues, former Director of Goa International Centre, deserves our thanks, as also Dattaraj Salgaonkar, a ranking industrialist for their local hospitality. Shri Pratap Singh Rane, the then Chief Minister of Goa, and his wife were gracious to receive the honourable guests at their official residence. Last but not the least, the Editor would like to thank all the teaching and non-teaching staff members of the Centre for their unstinting cooperation to make this Conference a success. On the whole, it has been a very fulfilling experience to all of us.

V. Shivkumar

Contents

List of Participants

Ali, Usman, H.E. High Commissioner of Trinidad & Tobago

Bharati, A., Lecturer, Baroda University

Borkar, D.V., Registrar, Goa University

Carvalho, J., Consul General of Portugal

D'Souza, Placido, India's Former Ambassador to Panama

Desa, E., Director, National Institute of Oceanography

Doctor, Adi, Professor of Political Science, Goa University

Figueroa, Uldaricio, H.E. Ambassador of Chile

Fr. Borges, Charles, Director, Xavier Institute for Historical Studies

Goberdhan, Danny, Business Consultant, London

Godrej, S.P., Chairman, Godrej & Co.

Gomes, O., Professor, Goa University

Halarnkar, T. D., Director, Students Welfare, Goa University

Kakodkar, A., Documentation Officer, Centre for Latin American Studies, Goa University

Kamat, Pratima, Reader in History, Goa University

King, Jocelyn K., H.E. Ambassador of Venezuela

Krishnan, N., Retd. Additional Secretary, Ministry of External Affairs, GOI

Kumar, Dilip, Director, CBI, Goa

Kumar, Rakesh, Joint Secretary, Ministry of External Affairs, GOI

Kumar, Shailendra, Deputy Secretary, Ministry of Commerce, GOI

Loundo, Dilip, Brazilian Studies Chair, Goa University

Mahale, K., Director, Institute of Indo-European Studies, Goa

Mathew, K.M., Professor of History, Goa University

Menezes, David, Industrialist, Goa

Narayanan, R., Professor, Jawaharlal Nehru University

Rodrigues, S.F., Executive Director, Goa International Centre

Rouch, M., Professor in French, Goa University

Salgaocar, Dattaraj, Industrialist, Goa

Sampietro, Elda B., H.E. Ambassador of Argentina

Sebastian, M.K., Scientist, Indian Space Research Organisation

Sharma, D., Managing Director, Goa Tourism Development Corporation

Shirodkar, P.P., Director, Goa Archives

Shivkumar, V., Director, Centre for Latin American Studies, Goa University

Singh, Dalbir, Research Associate, Centre for Latin American Studies, Goa University

Soares, Louis Filipe de Macedo, H.E. Ambassador of Brazil

Sonde, B.S., Vice-Chancellor, Goa University

Srinivasan, Gopal, Executive President, Zuari Agrochemicals Ltd.

Trias, Volga Chamero, H.E. Ambassador of Cuba

List of Student Participants

de Mello, Monica
Jayamohan, Smitha
de Cunha, Socorina
Lucia
Pradhan, R.P
Mehta, Shailendra
Rane, A.
Raposo, F.
Rodrigues, M.

1

India-Latin America-Caribbean Relations : Needed Direction for Study and Rescarch

*—B.S. Sonde**

Our Goa University's Centre for Latin American Studies (CLAS) has been planning and preparing for this important Conference for the past few months, under the active sponsorship and advice of the Ministry of External Affairs (MEA). I am very glad that finally we are all here today at the Inaugural Session of this Conference. First of all, I would like to greet all our guests, particularly, their Excellencies—Ambassadors from many Latin American and Caribbean countries, senior officials from the MEA and our distinguished Session Chairpersons and speakers, who have taken time off from their places of work and busy schedules to be with us at Goa University for this Conference. The prestigious Goa International Centre indeed provides us a fine setting and good ambience for our discussions at this Conference.

We are eagerly looking forward to the formal presentation of the key-note address by H.E. Uldaricio Figueroa, Ambassador of Chile in India and an equally important inaugural address to be presented by Mr. Rakesh Kumar, Joint Secretary, MEA, both on the theme topic, which would set the tone for the deliberations at this Conference. I am quite certain that the three sessions to follow focussing on recent developments in Latin America and Caribbean, bilateral issues, Indo-Latin American concerns, emerging trends in trade, commerce, industry, science, technology, education, research, travel and tourism etc. will provide an opportunity for a fruitful

* Professor B.S. Sonde is the Vice-Chancellor of Goa University.

discussion among the delegates. I am also certain that the Valedictory Session to be chaired by India's leading industrialist Shri. S.P. Godrej will facilitate a proper and fitting conclusion of the Conference and for drawing up of the Recommendations.

CLAS is a unique centre for Area Studies established by the University Grant Commission in Goa University. Teaching and research are pursued at this Centre, primarily relating to subjects such as Latin American History, Government, Political Economy, Sociology, Inter-American Relations, Latin America in International Politics and the like. Not only considerable expertise is built up in this Centre on socio-economic, cultural and political scenarios in Latin America and publications relating to these studies brought out regularly by the Faculty and students, but the Centre has also developed commendable contacts and joint programmes with scholars in these countries. This has enabled comparative studies and research on selected issues of relevance to India and Latin America and Caribbean.

We believe that Goa has the best credentials for launching, sustaining and expanding such a centre on Latin American Studies at an Indian University. Our long association with Iberian society, culture, literature, trade, politics, etc. ever since Vasco da Gama landed in Goa in 1498 affords us this unique characteristic. Although by and large, Indians have had a mind-set that Latin America is too far, too alien and too inaccessible for us in Goa, it has not been so. Moreover, in the last 50 years since Indian independence, there has been a gradual increase in India in understanding Latin America and we believe our CLAS has a crucial role in this—particularly in the coming years.

More recently economic reforms in many Latin American and the Caribbean countries and the economic liberalisation in India are bringing both these regions closer. Great advances witnessed in science and technology on the world scene and the growing interest all over the world to exploit these advances in our daily life have also brought up many challenges—particularly for India as well as the Latin American and the Caribbean countries, which are today categorised as developing countries. It is in this context, we attach special importance to this Conference on *Emerging Trends in Indo-Latin American and Caribbean Relations.* Our similarities as well as complimentary strengths in several areas should enable us to work out meaningful projects of interest to our regions through the discussions at this Conference. It is precisely for this reason, a full session dealing with industry, science and technology and related issues has been included in this Conference.

Recent advances in IT are binding together several nations, however distant they may be. Particularly software development has received much attention in India in recent years and the country has demonstrated its skills and capabilities in this area in a commendable way. We are told that there is now a major requirement of educational material and software in the Portuguese and Spanish language at all levels in Latin American countries, particularly in Brazil. Our strengths in Portuguese language in Goa and in software in India as a whole should enable us to work out suitable programmes here to support these needs in Latin America. We would welcome any ideas/ suggestions in this connection.

Latin American and the Caribbean diplomatic missions in India have shown keen interest in the activities of CLAS at Goa University. We have also a Brazilian Chair at our University established by the Government of Brazil. I am sure this Conference will strengthen these linkages further and also enable expanding our association in other areas like science, technology, industry and education. I hope the delegates will have a useful discussion and deliberations at the Conference. I will be eagerly looking forward to the recommendations of this conference. I congratulate Prof.V.Shivkumar and his dedicated team who had taken upon themselves the task of organising this Conference. I do hope the Centre would organise similar Conferences to continue this dialogue.

2

Perspectives on India-Latin America Relations

—*R. Narayanan**

Elite groups in India have long been accustomed to talk about the common problems and destinies of Asia, Africa and Latin America. Of these three continents, sharing in many respects common historical legacies and experiences, admittedly Latin America is geographically the farthest and therefore, afforded least direct contact. While these factors contributed to an attitude that was generally friendly and certainly devoid of any negative sentiments, they also resulted in a much slower awakening among the educated and other elite groups of the desirability of forging closer relations with countries of Latin America.

Yet, in the course of the past fifty years of its independence, India's relations with the Latin American countries have expanded significantly transcending mere exchange of formal diplomatic courtesies to encompass a variety of meaningful and purposive economic linkages. The pace at which these linkages have expanded, however, has been rather slow.

Beset as it was with its domestic as well as regional problems in the immediate aftermath of its independence, no doubt India paid little attention to the countries of Latin America beyond establishing diplomatic contacts. More basic to its disinclination in seeking closer ties with Latin America in these early formative years was the attitudinal reticence of India's ruling elite who given their long association with the

* R. Narayanan is Professor of Latin American Studies at Jawaharlal Nehru University, New Delhi.

British Commonwealth, perceived the Latin American region as part of the "sphere of influence" of the United States. No less important was the muted response of the leading countries of Latin America on some of the causes that India espoused in the incipient years of the Cold War.

Towards the end of the 1950s and early 1960s, however, India-Latin America relations began to warm up. Not only the rigours of the Cold War had reached new heights but the sensitivity of the developing countries including India and the Latin American countries to the new challenges had become more pronounced demanding concerted efforts on their part. At the bilateral level, it became evident in the first-ever visits of the presidents of Argentina and Mexico with whom India signed fresh trade protocols, and at the same time renewed its trade agreement of 1951 with Chile. Elsewhere, particularly in international fora such as the United Nations Conference on Trade and Development (UNCTAD), India and the countries of Latin America developed useful contacts. Unlike in the earlier years they even voted together in the United Nations in support of global disarmament, nuclear non-proliferation and peaceful use of nuclear energy. What is even more important from the point of view of India was Cuba's joining as a full member of the Non-aligned Movement (NAM) at its formal summit meeting at Belgrade along with Bolivia, Brazil and Ecuador attending the conference as observers.

Basic to these encouraging developments were the intrinsic socio-economic changes in Latin America, which saw the rise of an assertive middle class, a more organised labour movement and, above all, the advent of a revolutionary movement—all of which triggered the region's active role in regional and international affairs. Capturing the mood and moment of the region, Mexican philosopher and poet Octavio Paz graphically described:

> Our situation in Latin America is that of the majority of peripheral countries. For the first time in over three hundred years, we have ceased to be an inert material which the strong could use as they wished....And

> suddenly we have reached the limit; in these few years we have exhausted all the historical forms Europe could provide us. There is nothing left except nakedness or lies....Nakedness and defencelessness are awaiting us. But there, in that 'open' solitude transcendence is also awaiting: the outstretched hands of other solitary beings. For the first time in our history, we are contemporaries of all mankind.

Interestingly, the resurgence of economic nationalism resonating in the raging dependency discourse in Latin America around these years orchestrated well with the strident notes of Afro-Asian nationalism in the successive NAM concerts. Admittedly it augured for more positive Indian overtures towards Latin America. It is in these circumstances, India's prime minister Indira Gandhi in the course of a debate on foreign policy on the floor of the parliament propitiously announced her 'maiden' voyage to Latin America and added that Latin American countries

> share many ideals with us and we hope to do more to know each other better...in the past we had been a little too aloof with the Latin American countries. I realise that much more needs to be done.

And in less than five months following her statement she undertook her voyage to ten countries of the Latin American and Caribbean region and delivered as many as thirty-five formal addresses, in all of which she underlined the need for India and Latin America to come closer not only in view of the striking similarity in their socio-economic conditions but also because of their common and abiding commitment to world peace. Yet another constant refrain in these speeches underscored the imperative and urgent need to do away with the inequities between the developed and the developing countries and to formulate common strategies for abridging the gap between them.

As a sequel to the first-ever state visit of an Indian prime minister to the Latin American region, the government set up two diplomatic missions, one in Peru and, the other in

Venezuela, primarily to strengthen trade ties with those countries and also dispatched high-level trade delegations composed of the officials of the concerned ministries along with representatives of the business community. In subsequent years, not only earlier trade agreements with countries such as Argentina, Brazil and Chile were further strengthened, but fresh preliminary agreements with countries such as Colombia, Peru were initiated and signed before long. As a consequence, India's imports from Latin America registered a sudden and sharp spurt tilting the payment balance in favcur of the Latin American countries. Given that most Latin American countries in the decade of 1960 had adopted a conscious export-led growth strategy as against India's accent on growth-led exports, it is not surprising that the Indo-Latin American trade flows, however modest, underwent a swift change leading India to experience ever since an unfavourable balance *vis-à-vis* Latin America.

A more positive outcome at the bilateral level, however, was the initiative taken by India and some of the leading Latin American countries such as Argentina, Brazil and Mexico to forge closer cooperation in specific fields of science and technology. Accordingly, in mid-1975 India and Mexico ratified an agreement providing essentially for the exchange of technical and scientific data in identified economic sectors. Again, following India's successful detonation of a nuclear device, in May 1974, both Argentina and Brazil signed separately an agreement with India providing not only for cooperation in the peaceful uses of nuclear energy but also for exchange of information and scientists in the nuclear energy sector.

Concurrent with these developments, pointing to a future of increasing bilateral purposive cooperation between India and Latin America, was the acceleration of the process of multilateral cooperation and concerted common policy stance on a number of global issues between India and the leading countries of Latin America both within and outside the United Nations. Illustrative of these instances of cooperation are the increasing accession of Latin American countries in NAM, G-77 and G-15; and the leading role that India and the countries of Latin America have played in such international fora as the UNCTAD, the United Nations Conference on Law of the Seas (UNCLS), and the Six-nation Conference on Disarmament. Largely thanks to the joint efforts of India and Latin America such measures as the framework of generalised preferences for the less developed countries' manufactures and semi-manufactures as well as the shift away from the traditional three-mile limit for territorial waters to a formula of twelve miles together with an economic zone extending up to 200 miles came to be adopted in the UNCTAD and UNCLS respectively.

Convergence of interests and common policy posturing became even more apparent when, in mid-1970s, Latin America joined with India and the rest of the Afro-Asian countries in the UN General Assembly's approval of the declaration on the establishment of a New International Economic Order (NIEO) and an action programme on NIEO, which to some extent gave shape to the setting up of the South-South Commission eventually. Also, it was under the aegis of the NIEO such initiatives as indexation of raw material prices, creation of producer associations, national sovereignty over natural resources, regulation of transnational corporations and control of technology transfers—all with a view to bring about equitable redistribution of world resources—came to be adopted.

Having gone thus far on the road of multilateralism both under the auspices of the UN and outside, by the beginning of the decade of 1980, India opted for the course of deepening its bilateral relations with select Latin American countries with which it could intensify its relations not only for mutual advantage in respect of their global objectives but also for each other's specific economic needs. Based on these rationale, India identified three major continental-sized countries of the region—Argentina, Brazil and Mexico—with which it sought economic cooperation.

Among these three countries, India's relations with Mexico began moving significantly from one of uninvolved but correct diplomatic relations to reach meaningful economic cooperation and mature international partnership. Accent was placed not as much on commodity trade exchanges as strengthening bilateral economic cooperation in industry, agricultural development, food production, energy, science and technology, tourism, communication and financial cooperation. To this end, in 1962 an agreement was signed along with a protocol for the establishment of an Indo-Mexican Sub-Commission for financial cooperation to prepare new forms and evaluate existing forms of financial relations etc. Based on these instruments of economic cooperation the two governments set up at the official level a joint commission to review and assess periodically areas of industrial and technological collaboration.

One immediate and concrete outcome of these trend-setting instruments of economic cooperation purported to bring about transfer of technology was the signing of two specific contracts—one, between the Oil India Company and Mexico's PROTEXA, under which Mexican oil exploration agency was given a contract worth US $ 31 million with supporting credit for onshore drilling and ancillary service in the Mahanadi basin in the eastern state of Orissa; and the other, signed between Engineers India and Mexico's Instituto Petroleo to facilitate cooperation between the two. Instances of such useful economic cooperation essentially to share indigenously developed technologies between India and Mexico are mushrooming. Of these, one that merits mention is the sizeable investment that ISPAT Group of India has made in the Mexican steel production sector. Beginning with outright purchase of the Lazaro Cardenas steel plant when Mexico in the process of privatising the loss making public sector units, ISPAT since then has acquired interest in three more units in Mexico. ISPAT Mexicana (IMEXA), an affiliate of the ISPAT Group of India, is today Mexico's largest steel exporter and has just initiated the second phase of its expansion programme to increase liquid steel production and thereby strengthen its backward integration by increasing its self-sufficiency in metallics. On the reverse, while there are no major Mexican investment or joint ventures in India, negotiations are under way for such ventures with Mexican technology for the production of stainless steel and cement. Very recently, Tubo de Acero has entered into agreement with Indian government-owned Oil and Natural Gas Commission for production and supply of seamless pipes.

Similar initiatives with a view to evolve programmes of industrial cooperation with Argentina have been made in 1980s. Beginning with the signing of a preliminary trade protocol providing for the exchange of delegations, holding of periodic trade fairs and exchange of vital information on each other's development programmes, India and Argentina by mid-1980s signed yet another agreement which, among others, provided for the establishment of a joint commission to explore areas of industrial collaboration. These efforts have yielded some progress. Areas in which such technological cooperation have occurred include joint ventures in sugar refining, potable alcohol, chemicals used in textile industry, telecom sector, shipping containers, in all of which Argentine companies will collaborate with companies in India. Also, some Indian companies have set up ventures in Argentina for assembling and sale of motorcycles and manufacture of reactive dyes for cotton and silk yarns.

The third ranking Latin American country with which India is gradually moving closer on bilateral terms is Brazil. Convinced of their parallel experiences in respect of economic development, the two countries have been making efforts for some time to build two-way relations. Also, because both countries share similar views on a number of global economic issues, strengthening and expanding ties had even become imperative. It, therefore, posed no serious problems when overtures were made by both countries to seek meaningful cooperation. Beginning with the signing of two basic agreements—one, for trade exchanges and the other for exchange of nuclear know-how—way back in 1968, both countries have moved significantly in deepening their linkages. In discussions since, both have underscored the "benefits" that could accrue by developing collaboration in the sophisticated consultancy and engineering systems that obtain in both countries.

In line with this understanding, Indian and Brazilian companies have already launched joint ventures both in Brazil and India. In Brazil, an Indian engineering firm has set up a joint venture with its Brazilian counterpart to manufacture equipments in power transmission as also a similar venture for manufacture of pharmaceuticals. Both these ventures would cater not only to the domestic Brazilian market but also throughout Latin America. Two joint ventures set up in India with Brazilian collaboration are producing soya oil and meal of which one-third is exported to Brazil. Besides, there are other approvals of such joint ventures in other sectors, which are likely to go into production in the near future.

Obviously, India's strategy in respect of promoting economic relations with distant Latin American countries is not predicated on mere commodity exchanges. On the other hand, India is of the view that commodity exchanges based on conventional commercial transactions are rather premature and less promising notwithstanding the market surveys that seem to suggest rich and rewarding potentials. However scientifically done, mere market surveys by themselves do not immediately open up or provide for two-way trade exchanges. It calls for a number of other preliminaries, which, among others, include exposure to the market and other prerequisites such as shipping and credit facilities. What is more, as far as India is concerned, the accent in its development strategy is not as much hinged on export-led growth as it is on growth-led exports. India is also aware that the recent gyrations in the exchange value of East Asian currencies are likely to make the already highly subsidised Chinese exports more competitive *vis-à-vis* Indian goods in the Latin American markets.

It is for these considerations, India's economic strategy

towards Latin America is to seek gradually trade expansion through technology transfer and joint ventures either in host Latin American countries or third countries of the region. This has been the familiar pattern of at least countries such as Canada and Japan, which are the recent entrants in the Latin American markets. If trade transactions of major Latin American countries have increased substantially in recent years, it is because these countries, in association with the local entrepreneurs of the region have transferred their technology to Latin America. The presence of these joint enterprises in the mineral and manufacturing sectors makes it palatable for a number of Latin American countries to encourage two-way trade with countries with which they have launched joint ventures.

The literature on transfer of technology to developing countries on the enterprise-to-enterprise level strongly suggests that corporately owned US technology is the least adaptable to conditions prevailing in the developing countries. At best the industrially advanced countries adapt technology to market size, but practically they never adjust it to local factor proportions. There are good reasons for the US multinationals to do so. Given the highly protective Latin American markets, they do not want to complicate their own operational problems and readapt their technology. This being so, it offers immense opportunities for India, as it has offered to Canada and to some extent Australia in the recent past especially in Latin America, to enter into joint ventures in these parts of the world. What is more, an effort towards infusing indigenous Indian technology has, as recent experience shows, facilitated correcting the "folkloric" imageries of India in Latin America.

Whatever may be the imperatives, increasingly countries such as Brazil are becoming disenchanted with the prevalent export-led growth strategy for development. In time it is to be expected that many of these countries may have to opt for an inward-looking development strategy. Leading Brazilian economists in recent years have argued that the basic priority for continental-sized countries such as Brazil placed in a bind should develop the domestic market. Given that the capital goods industry is still at its formative stage, a deliberate policy to ensure technological advance based on transfer of technology for similarly placed countries, they argue, has become imperative. In other words, what is suggested is more or less the same that was advocated by ECLA in the 1950s seeking governmental participation in the industrialisation process—except now there is a much clearer suggestion as to what the state should be doing and in favour of whom, thus radically departing from the earlier ECLA prescription.

There is no gainsaying that policy shifts such as selective bilateralism and accent on technology tie-ups in specific sectors with the 'thrust' countries of Latin America were largely the result of a gradual change in India's overall developmental strategy. In fact, by 1985 it had become obvious that the past policy regime of planned economic development predicated on import substitution together with physical control mechanisms had not produced the desired results. Resultant thinking on the economic policy led to some major departures from the earlier regimes in several directions. Broadly speaking, the major components of the revised economic policy sought removal and relaxation of physical controls, restoration of competition, modernisation of industries with hi-tech bias and an ever-larger role for the private sector. Although this shift, from a strong inward-orientation to a moderate outward orientation accompanied by a shift away from physical control regime, led to a fairly high growth rate in the manufacturing sector, it also gave rise to certain strains on the Indian economy. One immediate fall-out of moderate liberalisation was the mounting trade deficit, reaching a level in the range of \$ 71.7 to \$ 93.6 billion in the 1980s with an all time record level accounting for a deficit of 3.4 per cent of GDP in 1988-89. Even the current account deficit shot up from \$ 21 billion in 1980-81 to \$ 77 billion in 1990-91. Admittedly, certain unpredicted external factors too contributed to the exacerbation of the impending economic crisis. Of these at least two merit mention—the sudden disintegration of the

Soviet Union with its attendant distortions on India's exports to the Eastern bloc countries, and the other was the swift pace at which the European integration process began moving to a point of a common commercial policy which in turn impacted unfavourably on India's exports to its traditional partners in the European Union—Britain and Germany.

It is at this critical juncture, India in early 1990s opted for a policy of economic liberalisation relying more on market-driven forces and on the integration of the Indian economy with the global economy. One important component of the reform package, among others, is trade liberalisation. Although the full impact of the trade liberalisation is yet to be realised, current trends suggest that in the short period of the last five years, Indian exports have made a remarkable recovery from a negative export growth in 1991-92 to 17 per cent plus annual growth since mid-1990s. Encouraged by such an impressive export performance, India is targeting to almost triple the exports by the end of the century from $ 26 billion to $ 75 billion.

Where do the Latin American countries figure in the larger context of India's economic liberalisation? Admittedly, the twin processes of global economic change and India's own liberalisation stance makes it imperative that the Latin American region is seriously explored. Fortuitously, for India the evolving political and economic developments in the Latin American region seem to augur well. Simultaneous to the unfolding of economic liberalisation process in India, Latin America too is presently undergoing a process of political and economic liberalisation and restructuring. The emerging democratic regimes in many of these countries of the region are favourably inclined towards India. Placed in a similar predicament, countries such as Brazil had reacted exactly the same way as did India in the Uruguay Round multilateral trade negotiations on issues such as the inclusion of services, trade related investment measures (TRIMS) and trade related intellectual property rights (TRIPS). Besides these encouraging developments the Latin American countries have regrouped themselves as sub-regional economic units such as NAFTA,

MERCOSUR, GRAN and the CARICOM.

In the backdrop of these developments, India has evolved an economic strategy towards Latin America, first in its totality, and then on the basis of in-depth analysis, a country-specific thrust identifying special areas of economic cooperation. In identifying countries for such a thrust, two factors have been underlined—one, the larger countries that offer opportunities for interaction in several sectors for joint ventures, consultancy contracts and transfer of technology agreements, and two, given the regional sub-groupings, India needs to focus precisely on countries which could provide the foothold for India for entering these trade blocs. Targeting US $ 1 billion exports to Latin America, last year the government has launched "Focus: Latin America" project in joint consultation with the apex chambers of commerce and industry and the other concerned export promotion agencies. The programme will concentrate on Latin America in general with added emphasis on the major trading partners of the region. Three major product groups have been identified—textiles, engineering products and chemical products as focussed product groups. Designed to catalyse and intensify trade exchanges with Latin America, an Indian exhibition is scheduled in March of this year in Mexico. Also, EXIM Policy initiatives and trade promotion measures have also been made to provide incentives for the Indian business community to explore Latin American markets.

While these are measures that are likely to expand trade exchanges between India and Latin America, current trends in this respect are very encouraging. During the last six years, India's bilateral trade has increased from US $ 474 million to $ 1.05 billion, representing a record increase of 30 per cent to reach US $ 485 million in the year 1996-97 alone.

Of this sizeable increase in exports to Latin America, MERCOSUR countries, especially Brazil and Argentina, rank as first. For instance, India's exports to Brazil reached its highest-ever and in the process for the first time India has achieved a trade surplus with that country. Chemicals and pharmaceuticals are the star performers in India's exports to Brazil. Besides, engineering goods, machine tools as well as consumer non-durables such as textiles, linen and jute products are registering promise in India's exports to Brazil. Whereas exports to Argentina too have increased, yet a sudden spurt in Argentina's exports to India in recent years has made the trade balance in favour of the former. Compared to Brazil, India's export basket to Argentina is even more diversified to include electronic goods and automobiles and parts as well as non-durables such as leather goods.

The growing volume of trade has encouraged the shipping company, United Arab-Clipper Services, the only direct shipping line from Mumbai to the MERCOSUR ports to introduce additional vessels. Shortly from now, as many as six cargo vessels will carry merchandise every fortnight to MERCOSUR countries. Besides, facilities for loading containers from India to Latin American destinations on the basis of transhipment at Singapore are already available.

Admittedly, policies of economic restructuring adopted by the Latin American countries as well as India have opened immense opportunities for expansion of not only bilateral trade and commerce but also of cooperation in several fields leading to transfer of technology and know-how. At the least, the immediate task could be expansion of trade, if for no other reason than to eliminate the existing trade deficits of India with the region. By identifying specific thrust area products in thrust countries—which are not only the major regional economies but also important for being leading members of the emerging regional trading blocs—India can in the long term carve out a niche for itself in the Latin American region. Given the comparable levels of development and complementarities between India and the thrust countries of Latin America, deepening of economic interaction has become imperative.

Be that as it may. There are several bottlenecks to realising the potential export growth. The first and foremost is the mindset of the exporters themselves that has grown from their operating for long under a protective shelter. The limitation also arises from the fact that present trading practices between India and Latin America do not allow adequate and timely feed-back. This pattern of trade is in no mean way responsible for the failure to generate demand for Indian goods as they generally sell under foreign brand names and trademarks. While the present incentive schemes for export-promotion are generally export friendly, yet it has not reached the bulk of the Indian exporters who belong to the small- and medium-sectors. Also, Indian export expansion just as anywhere is handicapped more by poor marketing than by the intrinsically poor quality of goods. Information gap stands above all as a hurdle in establishing contacts between the trading communities on both sides. Efforts towards overcoming these key deterrents will have to be initiated before long. What it calls for is the coordination of the initiatives of Indian business and export organisations and based on these initiatives a blueprint for a long-term strategy needs to be evolved and enforced.

3

Latin America's Historic Contributions to the World Community

*—Uldaricio Figueroa**

Few regions in the world have a centennial tradition in looking for a common stand over important issues as the region of Latin America. But the main problem has been the lack of adequate fora to discuss, to deal with and to reach agreement. When it has happened it was not very difficult to arrive at a common stand perhaps, because we have similar background. We have lived in the same political and social environments, with similar aspirations and confronting similar political and social challenges both domestic and regional.

The majority of our countries attained independence at the beginning of the last Century. Cuba achieved it at the dawn of this Century and the Caribbean countries some three decades ago.

Many of our most distinguished Founding Fathers spread throughout the continent ideas of unity, ideas of integration and ideas to establish a confederation. Leaders like Simón Bolívar, Francisco de Miranda, José de San Martín, Juan Egana, Pedro Vicente Canete, Juan Martínez de Rosas, Bernado de Manteagudo and also Henry Clay were great promoters of these ideas. These coincidences in aspirations advanced 180 years ago and were not ripe enough in the world of those days.

Since the very beginning of our independence we however, started to develop close relations among ourselves.

---

* Uldaricio Figueroa is Ambassador of Chile in India.

On one side, to create common juridical instrument to allow the development of our external relations and on the other side, to consolidate the process of independence from the aggressive policy of intervention of European nations against the new American Republics. There had been invasions, blockades, occupation of territories, annexations etc. The new nations were worried because they were unarmed to fight against them. Thereafter, we had to face the intervention of the United States.

Foreign policy is a result of a variety of situations a country confronts. Since the beginning we developed together an active foreign policy to resolve the problems we commonly faced. Conferences on various matters were conducted in succession since 1826. Initially, these were conferences either among three, among four or among five countries. Subsequently, the call for conferences was for all with full participation of Brazil. Step by step, we elaborated a regional juridical system and in many respects we were much ahead of the international community.

The jurist conference held in Lima in 1887 resulted in a Treaty on Intellectual Property, the first of its kind in the history of the world. Only nine years later was signed the Union of Berne on Intellectual Property. A South American congress on Private International Law was convened and marked the beginning of consideration of issues of common interests at the regional level.

In 1890, the International Union of the American Republics, the first regional organisation was established, the first ever political international organisation in the world. It was established precisely 28 years prior to the creation of the League of Nations in Paris. The first task assigned to the new union—the Pan-American Union was the elaboration of the Treaty of Arbitration for the Peaceful Settlement of Disputes. It is interesting to remember that at this juncture was also debated the establishment of a single currency in the region, the construction of a railroad cutting across the continent, the creation of an international bank in Washington with branches in every Latin American country. These are evidences of our interest to forge close cooperation amongst ourselves.

It was also the beginning of our initiative to deal multilaterally with the main issues in our regional relations. The Drago Doctrine was adopted by which was declared prohibition of imposition of any coercive measures by any nation-states for repayment of debt arrears.

Since the Havana Conference in 1928, active work was undertaken for peaceful resolution of disputes, diplomatic asylum—a tradition and institution well elaborated in the region; on extradition; on maritime neutrality; on rights and duties of states in the event of civil strife. A convention on civil aviation was drafted; the first Code on Private International Law was signed. A commission on women was established and five years later was signed the Agreement on Political and Civil Rights of Women. It was in this conference in 1928 that a treaty was signed establishing an international organisation of commerce to regulate the flow of trade amongst us. However, it failed to get the required ratification. Twenty years subsequently this treaty was taken as a main draft to elaborate in Geneva the United Nations effort at arriving at General Agreement on Tariff and Trade (GATT).

In 1938 in Lima was approved the Declaration in Defence of Human Rights, exactly nine years prior to the United Nations' initiative towards Universal Declaration on Human Rights.

But without any doubt, the principle of non-intervention has been the main pillar in our relations until now. Always, there existed a diversity of interests between the United States and the American Republics. Maintaining cordial relations has not been an easy task and this situation has contributed, and in some respects has been fundamental to the strengthening of unity among the Latin American countries.

The validity of the principle of non-intervention has been incorporated very deep in our foreign policies. We have elaborated this principle in such a way that no other people in the world today can claim it as fundamental as it is in our region. None can defend it with the force that we in Latin America do it.

At the beginning of the current decade and keeping in mind the immediate past political experiences, we incorporated in our model of day-to-day coexistence respect, observance and implementation of democratic norms and forms of government and a conviction not to recognise any change in the democratic order. An extensive debate was held last year on the need for sustaining democratic principles and governance. It ended at the Ibero American Summit with the "Declaration of Vina del Mar" signed by all Presidents and Head of States of Ibero America. Without doubt this political covenant is a milestone in broadening the democratic efforts in Latin America and the Caribbean.

Furthermore, all countries of the region in unison have supported the principle of full respect for human rights which is being monitored by the Inter American Commission of Human Rights and the Inter American Court of Human Rights.

Thus, non-intervention, democracy and human rights have today become the main pillars of the political relations among the Latin American countries.

The policy of consultation amongst us on matters of common concern is as yet an unachieved goal. The existing forum does not need the minimum requirements for such consultation. Many attempts have been made to set up ad hoc systems of consultation. They have failed largely on account of lack of follow-up initiatives.

The 1963 Alta Gracia meeting in Argentina was an effort towards coordinating our economic positions. The 1967 Vina del Mar meeting in Chile tried to move the consultation into political issues but again failed in its follow up action.

The Organisation of American States (OAS) is not a place for consultation or to debate problems seeking common agreements. For, OAS besides the Latin American and the Caribbean countries include the United States and Canada and therefore debating on these issues would mean confronting these countries whose interests are contrary to the rest of the continent.

The United Nations Economic Commission for Latin America and the Caribbean known as ECLA or CEPAL is supposed to be *for* Latin America and the Caribbean but we find there the United States, Canada, Spain, France, Netherlands and the United Kingdom. So, ECLA or CEPAL is not a forum *for* Latin America.

Despite these setbacks, countries of Latin America have continued their search for the best way to coordinate amongst themselves on major issues. A small group of nations known as the Contadora Group started in the 1980s to act in the region as a democratic group. Later on it was enlarged. In December 1986 in Rio de Janeiro it was decided to transform this group of countries into a permanent mechanism of consultation and political concertation. With that was born the Rio Group.

Today the Rio Group is the most important forum in the continent. Indeed, it is the coronation of a very long journey in the search of Latin America to have a forum to discuss its own problems and to have a real process of consultation and *concertación* in Latin America.

In general, our economic development followed the same pattern of inward development that most countries adopted after the Second World War with the all too familiar poor results. Last decade we faced a foreign debt crisis and economic stagnation. The media poetically christened it as "Latin America's Lost Decade". But countries of the region reacted and introduced structural changes orienting the economic process toward a free market economy. The actual activation of the economy of the continent is remarkable.

The perception in Latin America today is that the majority are moving through similar patterns of economic experiences. An intense economic transformation is underway. It is really a quiet and pacific revolution. Latin America has left behind its volatile past with high inflation, erratic economic policies and unmanageable external debt. Today, the continent is one of the most stable and viable economic zones in the world.

Last year according to ECLA, the economic recovery of Latin America and the Caribbean in 1996 showed a growth of 3.5 per cent as a whole and total exports of the continent was around US $ 240,000 million. The average inflation in the continent was around 20 per cent and the inflow of foreign capital stood at US $ 50 billion. These data give an encouraging picture of the current situation in the continent.

Around 35 years ago, new nation-states emerged in the continent, mainly in the Caribbean region with different traditions, languages and interests. Despite these differences Latin America and the Caribbean have begun to walk together. At the beginning we were in the process of discovering each other like any newly wed couple. We have realised that we have not only many things in common and have the same goals to achieve in the future. So we have developed a strong desire to live together and share the destiny of the continent.

In many countries generally speaking, there still persists the image of Latin America as a continent of political and economic instability. The evolving democratic process, the increasing respect and adherence to the principle of human rights and the gravity of the Rio Group and its significant role in world affairs and finally the irreversible process of economic restructuring are aspects changing the popularly held view of the continent.

Just like we use the barometer to measure weather, there is a yardstick to measure the resilience of a country or of a geographical area. Nobody invests in places where there is no stability or a degree of uncertainty about its future. Inflow of fifty billion of foreign capital is a solid amount and a very valid measure of the confidence reposed on Latin America by the international community.

4

India-Latin America Relations : An Overview

—*Rakesh Kumar**

As the countries of the world are moving on the road of globalisation, neither India nor the countries of Latin America can remain committed to the rationale of collective self-reliance. In the fast-changing world of today, countries are undergoing transformation by burying historical animosities and forging together for collective advancement. Even in the industrialised world national identities are getting blurred. We in India, fully conscious of the imperatives of the contemporary world have taken certain steps to achieve the goal of collective advancement in our immediate neighbourhood. Guided by this principle, we within the South Asia region are engaged in an effort to reshape our relations in the region in order to provide durable and peaceful environment for socio-economic progress of the society at large. India's stature in size and strength cannot be divested from the quality of relations that we have to evolve with our neighbours.

Since the advent of the United Front government, five major principles guide India's relations with its immediate relations—one, India will seek no reciprocity from its neighbours; two, no country of the region should allow its territory to be used against the interest of another country in the region; three, none of the countries of the region should interfere in the internal affairs of another; four, all countries of the region must respect each other's sovereignty; and five,

* Rakesh Kumar is Joint Secretary, Ministry of External Affairs, GOI.

all disputes have to be settled through negotiations. India is convinced that these five principles will help strengthen South Asia regional integration. In fact, the positive virtues of this collective approach is already evident in our relations with our neighbours. For example, resolution of outstanding issues relating to sharing the waters of Ganga by India with Bangladesh enjoined in a treaty has greatly enhanced bilateral relations. Similarly, the Mahakali Treaty with Nepal has opened up tremendous potentials for economic cooperation between India and Nepal. As regards Pakistan, we remain committed to build a relationship of trust, friendship and cooperation with a view to resolve all outstanding issues through multilateral negotiations on the basis of the Simla Agreement. To create a positive atmosphere and promote people-to-people relations, India has taken number of steps unilaterally such as issuing visas to the nationals of Pakistan and providing for active interaction amongst intellectuals, journalists and academicians of both countries. India is firmly of the view that promotion of people-to-people contacts and enhancement of trade and commercial ties would contribute to lay the foundations on which constructive relations between the two could develop. There is enough economic space in the region for both India and Pakistan to share and we are of the view that economic interaction between the two countries should be perceived not as an effort towards domination as much as to enrich opportunities for collective economic development.

Another important and immediate neighbour of India is China, with which we have over the years been able to overcome the differences which bedevilled our relations. New beginnings have been made. President of China, Xiang Zemin was in New Delhi a couple of months ago during which important bilateral agreements were signed. Basically, these agreements relate to evolving confidence-building measures in respect of security, which in turn have paved the way for working towards constructive ventures in the coming new century.

Although the regions of Latin America and the Caribbean are geographically distant India however, greatly values its interaction with these regions. In fact, India's policy towards the region has in recent years been not only to strengthen wider relations but put more economic content into them. India perhaps has the largest diplomatic representation among the Asian countries with the exception of Japan in South America—India has 13 missions in the region besides a number of consulate offices. Last year yet another consulate office in Sao Paulo was opened. Exchange of official visits between India and Latin America has continued over the last few years. President of India was in the region on a state visit in 1995. In the following year, prime minister of Trinidad and Tobago, Vasudev Pandey was the honoured guest on India's Republic Day. Besides, foreign ministers of Venezuela and Costa Rica, the speaker of the national assembly of Cuba and other high-ranking officials and leaders were received the same year.

In the realm of economic relations, India has not as yet fully exploited the potential that exists in the region. Although, India-Latin America trade has registered some increase during the past five years, it has not achieved the potential that it should. While India's exports in 1991-1992 amounted to 205 crores of rupees, during the last eight months of 1996 it has increased four times. Similarly, India's exports for the same period have increased from Rs. 855 crores to about Rs. 1400 crores. Major destinations of India's exports in the region are Brazil, Mexico, Chile and Argentina. Similarly India's imports in the region also came from these four countries.

Admittedly, India is looking for new possibilities of widening the net in manufacturing sectors like software and commercial vehicles. Already India's Tata Company has appointed an agent in the region to market their vehicles as well as software.

Undoubtedly, there is a need to educate the business community on both sides about the potentiality which exists and the complementarity of trade and commerce so as to exploit further the opportunities. In line with this strategy efforts are afoot to set up Chambers of Commerce to look into trade and venture capital potentials in both India and Latin America.

Regarding other significant aspects of Indo-Latin American relationship, given that both have been victims of terrorism, both share common concern on the growing incidence of terrorism. Also, India has taken note of the American efforts at dictating terms to the Latin American countries including the latest instance of the Helms-Burton Law, which has placed hurdles on Cuba's trade with third countries. Efforts are also on to put in place institutional linkages with regional organisations of Latin America. In this regard the linkages that have been made with the Rio Group and with Central American countries are important. India has also sought observer status, which has now been accepted by the Association of Caribbean states. Similarly, India is seeking such linkages with MERCOSUR, CARICOM and other regional organisations. In fact, India's foreign minister has been invited for discussion in some of these forums. In this connection, it may be mentioned that India has been attending the meetings of the Organisation of American States as observer for a long time.

Given the presence of large population of Indian origin of the countries in the Caribbean region, India is making efforts to build bridges culturally and economically with these countries. We have set up cultural centres in George Town, Guyana, Paramaribo, Surinam as well as last year in Port au Spain, Trinidad and Tobago. Yet another aspect which has brought the Caribbean close to India is the game of cricket. In fact, one of India's skipper, Robin Singh, comes from the Caribbean and his grandfather still lives there. Similarly, there is an association in Brazil of people from Goa. This kind of a resource needs to be fully exploited and used, be it in the business sector, the government or in the field of academics.

5

Evaluation of India-Argentina Relations

*—Elda B. Sampietro**

India-Argentina relations are multifaceted, encompassing different aspects including political, trade, cultural and cooperation in science and technology. Each of these aspects has a framework and these have been evolved by the policies of the governments of both countries through sustained and serious consultations. Important among them are the visits of Argentina's president Carlos Menem in 1994 in New Delhi and prime minister P.V. Narsimha Rao to Buenos Aires in 1995. Following these high level meetings, both sides had extensive bilateral consultations. In principle, these consultations have given a framework identifying the objectives and aims on the basis of which both countries have been engaged in pursuing their relationship. The most important of these objectives has been in the realm of trade and economic cooperation. Admittedly, the evolving economic relations between India and Argentina have been very encouraging. Two-way trade between the two in the past years has reached a US $ 100 million mark. Between 1995 and 1996 Argentina-India trade has increased by another US $ 200 million. Of the goods traded by Argentina one positive export item is edible oil. Besides, Argentina's major exports are seamless pipes for the exploitation and exploration of oil. Besides two-way trade, both are making efforts to develop investments. In fact, Argentine companies have shown much interest in certain areas such as importantly, telecommunications. Further, Argentina has both experience and potentials in providing support for hydroelectric power generation. Keeping these in

* Elda B. Sampietro is Ambassador of Argentina to India.

view, relations between the two countries should develop towards establishing joint ventures. Yet it may be mentioned, such a task is not as easy and sustained efforts therefore will have to be made to go beyond establishment of medium level joint ventures.

Despite efforts at deepening economic linkages, the progress has not been satisfactory. It is for these considerations the Chambers of Commerce of both countries have begun seeking cooperation through memorandum of understanding (MoU) such as the Chamber of Commerce of Buenos Aires with the Chamber of Commerce of Bombay and the Confederation of Indian Industries with the Union Industrial of Argentina. It is through these institutional linkages, it would be possible for both countries to go beyond mere trade relations. In this respect, the Indian delegation from Gujarat besides FICCI and CII visiting Buenos Aires recently has greatly enhanced prospects for Indo-Argentine economic cooperation. From the Argentine side, several individual businessmen have been visiting India with different interests and objectives. Besides, in 1996 seminars were held in Buenos Aires and Rosarío on India. No less than 50 medium- and small-sized Argentine companies evinced incredible interest in India and its development. Ever since they are looking towards identifying reliable Indian partners to sign joint ventures. Admittedly, this has been a positive exercise. The same can be said of India too and the positive sign in this respect is India's participation in the Buenos Aires trade fair last year. While these are encouraging trends in Indo-Argentine trade relations, yet there are other possibilities that needs to be explored.

Besides trade, mention needs to be made about bilateral cooperation in science and technology. In 1985, a treaty on cooperation in science and technology was signed by both providing for exchange of information, personnel etc. It is possible to enlarge the scope of this treaty by incorporating universities of higher learning and research institutes.

Although the history of cooperation between India and

Argentina in the fields of science and technology is long, it is time that efforts are made to identify specific areas which among others include computer software and mining. Mining is not well developed in Argentina and there is potential for India to help assist in this respect. Similarly, India's Silicon Valley in Bangalore could open up opportunities for cooperation. Just as much, Argentina has certain capabilities which could be offered especially in the sectors of agriculture and industry. The National Institute of Agriculture and the National Institute of Industry and Technology of Argentina could extend cooperation besides universities and research institutes in areas such as food processing and so on.

In the cultural field, it is a matter of pride for Argentina to promote the country's artists and their art forms and Argentina has had in the past useful cultural exchanges with India. Yet, the scope for the deepening of cultural ties is immense and efforts will have to be made to exchange scholars and artists on the basis of an agreed framework between the two countries.

6

Economic Profile of Chile and Prospects for Indo-Chilean Cooperation

—*Uldaricio Figueroa**

Political, social and economic stability consolidated at the beginning of 1990s with the restoration of democracy has provided Chile a solid foundation for uninterrupted growth and for spreading its benefits to even larger segments of its population. This has been possible because of the maintenance through the years, by different governments of consistent economic policy and strategies.

The changes in the economic sphere have brought about substantial modifications in the country's productive structures. It has transformed Chile from a closed economy with high levels of protection to an open economy well situated to take advantage of opportunities in external markets.

Among the structural changes, those which stand out are trade and financial liberalisation, internal market liberalisation, pension system reforms, privatisation and labour reforms, all of which have fostered an environment of greater efficiency and international competitiveness.

The unilateral opening up to external trade, supported by an active policy of bilateral, regional and multilateral agreements has enabled Chile to progressively increase its level of trade which in turn has fuelled the country's competitiveness abroad. In this manner, the country has achieved a steady growth in exports of goods and services. While exports are still closely linked to natural resources, they are currently diversified at the levels of both products and

* Uldaricio Figueroa is Ambassador of Chile to India.

markets. Moreover, with low levels of protection—the tariff is only 11 per cent ad valorem—and with no non-tariff barriers to trade, the economy has become an increasingly attractive market for new products and sophisticated technologies. We have eliminated hidden regulations which obstructed imports and removed arbitrary intervention of the bureaucracy more often delaying the import procedures.

So, we have opened our market. The Chilean market is not a big one. We are a small country. We are a market of medium-high per capita income of around US $ 5000. Our imports last year amounted to US $ 17 billion, almost a half of the total imports of India. Though India is 66 times bigger than Chile in terms of population, in terms of imports it is twice as large.

The following figures give an illustration of the present economic trends of Chile: the average economic growth in the last five years has been 7.6 per cent; national savings rate during the same period has been 26 per cent of the GDP, one of the highest in the developing countries; realised foreign investments for the same period has been in the order of over US $ 4 billion and last year alone it stood at US $ 6 billion; and the composition of the foreign debt kept changing in its structure. (A decade ago Chile's foreign debt—Government debt or government guaranteed debt—was 100 per cent; today the private sector has 75 per cent of all the foreign debt without government guarantee. So much so, the residual 25 per cent of foreign debt belonging to the public sector represents only four months of the average exports of Chile.

As regards bilateral trade between Chile and India, the trend has been what could be described as a disparity in opportunities. There does not exist reciprocity on the Indian side. This is the result of the disparity in the economic policies adopted in both countries.

Chile is offering to India an open market without restrictions or discriminations. On the other side, Chile confronts an Indian market with restrictions.

India can sell in Chile any kind of products but we produce

and manufacture domestically leather, rugs and pharmaceutical products and we do not impose any restrictions on India so as to protect the domestic production. We do assemble cars and trucks in Chile with a high percentage of national spare parts and India too is selling cars and trucks in Chile. We have a textile industry but this is not a reason to prohibit the imports of textiles from India. Our policy of restructuring the economy and liberalisation of trade is intended to help facilitate Chilean domestic production to compete with foreign production and it is the Chilean consumer, not the government who should choose between the domestic and foreign products according to price and quality. This in substance is the policy rationale of our liberalisation.

In the last four years, Indian exports to Chile have grown from US $ 12 million in 1993 to 21 million in 1994 and 34 million in 1995. Last year, India increased its exports to Chile by 70 per cent reaching the all-time high of US $ 58 million.

What happened with the Chilean imports to India? India has always bought from Chile minerals, mainly copper and continued to do so and will continue to do so for many years ahead regardless of whatever economic policy India adopts. The trend to buy Chilean minerals therefore, is likely to continue to be the same as before.

India's economic liberalisation policy in respect of external trade has merely offered Chile entry in the Indian market of raw materials such as fish meal, raw timber, wood pulp and tartaric acid.

In the past four years, while India has increased its exports of manufactured products, consumer products and ready made goods to Chile worth US $ 12 to 70 million, Chile has increased its exports to India, excluding copper, but including all other minerals from US $ 4 to 14 million only. Last year, Chile's total exports to India did not increase over the previous year. In 1995 and 1996, the total amount was the same, while India increased its exports to Chile by 70 per cent. The Indian market remains closed with many restrictions affecting the Chilean products.

Trade relations of India with Chile are very far from the reality of the principle of reciprocity. Perhaps the best way and the most appropriate forum to analyse and to discuss this trend and the application of non-tariff barriers to the Chilean products, should be the World Trade Organisation.

The different levels of development, the different types of natural resources, the development of technology that each country has and the political will to share it with other country the particular advantages it enjoys, make it possible to establish a degree of cooperation. The economy does not operate in a political vacuum. The economic cooperation has a political dimension.

It is praiseworthy that the Government of India's Ministry of External Affairs and the University of Goa have taken the initiative to examine the best possible and concrete way to set up collaborative exercises. As Chile and India enjoy an excellent degree of political understanding and share many of the political values, it is possible, with good will, to establish a solid cooperation.

As far as Chile is concerned, most of the activities are in the private sector. That means that it is up to them to decide to enter into a degree of cooperation or joint venture. Mention of some areas where Chilean enterprises may have interest to explore a sort of cooperation with India can be made.

(a) Almost one-third of Chile, the extreme north, is desert, arid with scarcity of water. The hydroelectricity is brought from the Andes, hundreds of kilometres away. To provide energy to people and industries of this zone is a complex task. India is very well advanced and has developed its own technology in the area of solar energy. This is an area where it is possible to develop cooperative ventures.

(b) Another instance of cooperation is related to the application of nuclear energy, where India is very well advanced. There are several applications that Chile may profit from the high technology that India has.

Other areas of collaborations are in the application of atomic energy in the field of medicine, in the treatment of agro-industry, in the treatment of sewage, processing of garbage etc.

(c) Chile is testing its own satellites for scientific purposes which indeed offers possibility of cooperation with the Indian space research programme. While it is difficult to identify the different areas for fruitful cooperation in this field, it might be interesting that efforts are made to launch Chilean satellite from Indian soil.

Reciprocally, India too can benefit by Chilean enterprises. Of them, following merit mention.

(a) In Chile, the mining sector represents one of the major areas of its economy and the principle focus of investments. Chile being the first copper producer and the principal producer of other minerals like molybdenum, renium and lithium has developed a highly competitive mining industrial sector with modern technology and high quality products. Also, it has a high degree of technological development in mining activities such as exploration, exploitation and processing of ores and minerals. This is an area where it is possible to look for ways of cooperation.

(b) India has great potentialities in the area of fruits, whether fresh or processed. Chile has some experience in this field, especially in processing and packaging. With its exports of more than 200 million cases of fresh fruit annually, Chile has attained very high efficiency in the packaging sector.

(c) In the area of software, Chile and India are developing very fast, each one in its own way. India has attained strength and prestige. In Chile, the software industry is a fast growing sector at a rate of over 80 per cent a year. Two years ago, the total sales of software reached US $ 200 million and the exports of software last year

was around 50 million. More than 200 companies of all sizes are engaged in the software sector. Undoubtedly, this sector offers prospects for mutual cooperation specially in imparting training, workshops and exchange of visits to learn from mutual experiences.

Chile and India have developed very good political relations. Needless to state, real and solid partnership in bilateral trade and strengthening the cooperation in areas of common interest is now a mandatory duty for both countries. It is encouraging that both countries are working in this direction and fruitful harvest of the evolving cooperation can be best attained by both treating each other as equal partners with attendant reciprocity.

7

Bilateral Relations between India and Cuba

—*Olega Chamerro Trias**

Only five years ago many people affirmed that Cuba would not be able to withstand the collapse of the socialist governments. In 1993 the gross national product had decreased to 35 per cent in relation to the year 1989. Import had fallen by 75 per cent and the state budget deficit was in a proportion of thirty five per cent in relation with the gross national product. In 1994 the economic decline stopped and grew by a modest 0.7 per cent. In 1996 and 1997 the economy grew by 7 per cent. During 1996 the Cuban strategy to strengthen and promote its own dynamic internal developments were consolidated. One of the most solid basis of this consolidation has been the process of financial balance that the country has been creating since 1994. The performance of the Cuban economy last year can be evaluated as positive especially as the Cuban economy grew from the targeted growth of five per cent to 7.8 per cent. This achievement is very favourable in comparison to the rest of the countries of the region which has a growth rate of about three per cent. Also, there has been an annual over-valuation of the national currency. Contributing to this was the deposits which represented two per cent of the gross domestic product. As part of this economic transformation was the growing number of joint ventures with foreign countries which went up from 212 to 260 between 1995 and 1996 despite the blockade and the Helms-Burton Law. This has not happened by sheer accident. The survival of the Cuban economy owes it to the capacity of resistance of the Cuban people and their decision

* Olega Chamerro Trias is Ambassador of Cuba to India.

to overcome problems and withstand difficulties. It also reflects the social solidarity of the Cuban people as well as the political consensus which facilitated adjustments and changes that have been sometimes even painful.

Important changes are taking place in the Cuban economy. During the last five years, the decentralisation of Cuba's external trade is one of them. In the earlier period, only few were involved in Cuba's foreign trade. Today more than 150 organisations are engaged in the external trade sector of Cuba. For the first time in 1986 Cuba enacted a decree law, which allowed foreign investments in the domestic economy. Later in 1992, yet another law was approved. As a consequence of which Article 23 of Cuba's Constitution has been amended. Finally, in September 1995 a new investment law has been promulgated. In 1990, joint ventures existed only in the tourism sector and capital invested was only US $ 100 million. Today more than 260 joint ventures have been signed and the total investment is estimated around US $ 2 billion.

These transformations are noteworthy if one takes into consideration the fact that Cuba had been blockaded for the last 37 years and stringent legislations of the United States punish those who sought to invest in Cuba. However, the recent investment law promulgated by Cuba in 1995 is modern and a more precise legal device adopted to the reality of the present global economy. After all, it is vital to maintain and strengthen international linkages both in respect of the business in the financial sectors. The scope of the current legislation is directed towards extending economic collaboration based on foreign investment which at the same time would protect and safeguard the country's national resources. A new law makes the entire process of investment in Cuba more flexible and provides clear evidence of a legal basis ensuring confidence and security to the foreign investors. Besides, it contains guarantees such as non-expropriation, compensation in the final stages of the joint venture and repatriation of profit and capital and also an option of selling the equity at any point of time in the collaboration. All these are important to provide the right climate for foreign investment.

On the other side, further changes have been introduced in the economy without compromising the political and social character of Cuba's developmental process and without ushering in a new liberal policy in the country. So much so, the transition has been less traumatic. On the positive side, during the last five years thanks to the new investment and economic policies not a single school or hospital has been given away nor has anyone been cast aside as destitute in the streets. It is imperative to continue the social welfare measures of the past at least until the time a review of the state apparatus is completed. Yet, under the new dispensation the state has been able to provide work for more than 500,000 people who are involved in different economic sectors and activities.

Be that as it may, during the decade of 1980 the economic relations between Cuba and India were very encouraging and the total value of India-Cuba trade accounted for about US $ 25 million. In 1991-92, largely on account of the domestic economic situation in Cuba, India's trade with Cuba declined by US $ 7 million and presently it is minuscule. In the area of science and technology Cuba and India had been collaborating since 1976 and both have been exchanging experts and trainees in this area. To that extent, it can be said that both have made effective use of their respective scientific and technological capabilities. In this connection, the Indo-Cuban collaboration in the field of solar energy merits mention. Cuba has committed itself to the Government of India on collaborative ventures especially in the technology sector and to this effect Cuba has recently signed an agreement with India in Havana. Needless to state that besides shared political concerns, there is a great deal of opportunities that obtain for India-Latin America relations based on the dynamics of "South-South" cooperation. It is time that we overcome our traditional approach of seeking cooperation with the industrially advanced "North" and "West" countries. Latin America and the Caribbean today is not what it was 25 years ago and any international documents signed with these countries works out to the mutual benefit of the signatories.

To make collaborative ventures a reality, bilateral agreements should be signed and the details and concrete proposals worked out between the parties should include the cultural field as well. For instance, it may be possible to invite Cuban teachers to impart training in Spanish language to the Goa University's Centre for Latin American Studies. Similarly, over time it may be possible to meet the needs of the Centre through such cultural agreements.

8

Perspectives on Peru-India Economic Relations

—*Carlos Higueras Ramos**

Peru is a medium-sized nation with a small population. However, it is rich in resources that have been exploited for the country's development. It is also a country rich in traditions and customs which have been retained, much like in India since the most ancient times. Although most nations possess a rich cultural heritage, there are a few countries like Peru which show the diverse cultural and physical traits such as languages, races, culture and complex geographical contours harmoniously adapted and blended. Undoubtedly, these characteristics have made Peru a fascinating country and one of the greatest civilisations of mankind. Of these, three need to be underlined—one, the delicate balance of geography and space, the creativity and precision of work and the strong native Indian presence embodied in powerful values and systems of tradition and beliefs, making it a free society which is at the same time heterogeneous, modern and cosmopolitan. These are also the elements that give substance to contemporary Peru upon which depends much of its strength it needs to face the challenges of the future.

Needless to state, only less than six years ago, Peru was politically unstable with fiscal problems and an excessively interventionist legislation. Today, these have either vanished or at least been substantially abridged thanks to a remarkable effective economic and social stabilisation programme initiated

* Carlos Higueras Ramos is Ambassador of Peru to India.

by the government of president Alberto Fujimori who took up office in 1990.

Peru enjoys social peace and a well-endowed system of democratic institutions and has returned to the international community regaining the confidence of countries overseas especially in economic terms. All this has been due to a macro-economic equilibrium, free-market competition guiding the allocation of resources in the economy, ensuring equal treatment and open access to foreign investors in the operation of the economy, free from excessive regulations, subsidies, monopolies and artificially maintained high prices, open foreign trade, with drastic reduction on the average customs tariff from 66 to 15 per cent and especially by the privatisation of state owned companies. These measures have allowed Peru to improve the living standards of its people through the revitalisation of its economy offering attractive opportunities for the business community. What is of importance is the national and foreign private and state companies in Peru, by defining their corporate strategies and objectives have played a key role in the revitalisation of the economy. To illustrate, let me add that in the past two years investments in Peru amounted to a total of US $ 6.5 billion. Communications, energy and mining sectors were considered the most attractive by the foreign and national investors, with Spain, China, United Kingdom, Chile and the United States as the prime investors, this, notwithstanding the current hostage crisis in the Embassy of Japan in Lima. Beginning in 1991, Peru has successfully achieved its objective of modernising its economy through privatisation and on the basis of the lessons learnt, it intends to deepen the process of privatisation for the next five years.

Relations between India and Peru began on the afternoon of 26 March 1963, almost 34 years ago, when India completed 16 years of its independence and Peru 142 years. Until then, India was known to us as the land that Columbus never arrived to, and Peru represented the glorious past of the Incas. Ever since, we had many years of experience on the road of freedom, independence and solidarity and have been fighting together against an unjust world order, mainly in the cultural and economic spheres, and through our mechanism of defence, in the United Nations, the Group of 77 and the Non-Aligned Movement (NAM), and through our universities and centres of study both countries have experienced many important changes in the national and international arena.

Be that as it may, India-Peru two-way economic relations began gathering momentum. India's exports to Peru touching a comfortable US $ 50 million mark in 1991 as against imports of reaching US $ 1.5 million from India, five years later in 1996, the trade balance is showing a tendency in favour of India with India exporting goods worth US $ 25 million to Peru and Peru exporting goods worth US $ 3 million only. Although it is the respective commerce ministries of both countries that have to deal with the trade balance deficit with India, it is imperative that both should foster trade relations on the basis of equality and reciprocity. By increasing the volume and value on both sides, both can achieve better levels of trade taking into consideration the open and indiscriminate trade policy adopted by Peru towards world market including India.

But the new mechanism that India has put into force could permit Peru to take advantage of the potential of the Indian market and overcome the hindrances of present export import policy of India which has been in force since 1 April 1992 and shall continue to do so till 31 May 1997. Needless to add, India's export-import policy, among others, includes quantitative restrictions and high tariffs on extensive lists of products that India can import but which are classified as "prohibited", "restricted" or "canalized". This constitutes a problem to Peruvian exporters who greatly desire to be actively present in the commercial statistics of India.

Besides the potential for substantial bilateral trade, there exist many possibilities of economic interaction like joint ventures in different areas where India has a special interest or expertise. Yet, these potentials could not be exploited largely on account of the reckless management and finances which have put a majority of the state owned companies in dire crisis. Indeed, lack of clear objectives, stunted growth due to procedural controls rather than result oriented management and severe capital drains because of absurd across-the-board subsidies are the main problems plaguing the state-run corporate sectors. It is against this background in 1991 privatisation appeared as the available tool to carry out the much-needed turn-around. In spite of an extremely adverse and unstable political and economic environment. Peru has succeeded during the last five years in privatisation deals which have reached the mark of over US $5.5 billion, encompassing all sectors of the economy with communications, electric power generation, mining, finance, oil, transport, fisheries and tourism as the most favoured industries. This has permitted the state to utilise these investments for the social sector in terms of development projects and other ameliorative measures. The main result of these policy devices has been the substantial progress in the citizen participation programme to expand community-wide ownership in companies where the state is still a shareholder. More equitable wealth distribution across the nation, increased domestic savings, new and attractive investment opportunities, a broad based market, education, and a healthy image abroad may result from a full-scale Citizen Participation Programme.

In that sense, the situation in Peru has greatly improved as against the beginning of 1990 when the country had one of the worst economies in the world with high rates of inflation, massive fiscal and trade deficit without any internal development.

Regarding Peru and India, it may be said that there are similarities. For one, the physical appearance of the people of Peru and India are strikingly alike. It is true that languages and religions of the two countries are different, yet customs and outlook on life are more or less the same.

Today Peru is one of the countries where foreign companies can own plantation lands. It will even be possible for foreign investors to obtain land concessions for limited period of time.

Peru thus offers excellent business opportunities for Indian capital investors and enterprises. Besides the mining and fishery sector, the export-oriented manufacturing sector represents a good option for Indian investors since they can take advantage of Peru's free industrial world. Preferential treatments accorded by the European Union and the United States has given definite commercial advantages to them in Peru. Generalised system of preferences offered to Japan and to the Latin American countries has made Peru a very attractive place for any foreign oriented investment.

In sum, in the last six years Peru has experienced a revolution that has renewed domestic and foreign optimism in its future. Today, thanks to the progress and initiatives undertaken by Peru to return to the fold of the international financial community and to a legal framework of attractive laws and opportunities, investors have begun to clearly perceive that the advantages in Peru greatly outweigh any risk. Proof of the growing interest in the future of Peru is apparent in the recent official visits of the prime minister of China Li Peng, Malaysia's prime minister Mohamed Mahatir, Thailand's deputy prime minister Anmuay Viravan, Japanese premier Ryutaro Hashimoto and a host of business representatives of India. Above all, on the fiftieth anniversary of India's independence president of Peru Alberto Fujimori will be the state guest. All these, it is hoped would strengthen and foster closer bilateral relations making a future for India and Peru to be partners and friends.

9

Opportunities for Trinidad and Tobago-India Bilateral Relations

—*Usman Ali**

Trinidad and Tobago and India are currently poised to go beyond their historical and cultural relations. India's relations with Trinidad and Tobago began with the arrival on 13 May 1845 of the first wave of Indians who were brought by the British as indentured labourers to work in the sugar plantations when there was a scarcity of labour following the emancipation of slaves. Thanks to this, Trinidad and Tobago is one of the countries in the western hemisphere where there is a sizeable population of Indian origin (42 per cent). Another 40 per cent are of African origin and the rest is a mélange of people of European, Chinese, Middle East and mixed descent. Other countries in the region with sizeable people of Indian origin are Guyana and Surinam.

Manifestation of the strengthening and deepening of the close relations between Trinidad and Tobago and India was recently witnessed with the visit of the prime minister of Trinidad and Tobago, Basdeo Pandey as a special guest of the government of India to commemorate the Republic Day festivities in January this year. He was accompanied by a large business delegation and a cultural troop representing Trinidad's diverse culture and showcasing the country's unique contribution to the world of music—the steel band. A trade agreement and several memoranda of understanding in areas such as agriculture, low cost housing, and small-scale industries

* Usman Ali is the High Commissioner of Trinidad and Tobago to India.

were signed during the visit. It will be of interest to know further that cultural cooperation and science and technology cooperation agreements were signed in 1969 and 1985 respectively.

Until about 15 years ago, relationship between both countries was characterised essentially by the deepening of cultural ties manifested in the visits of Indian artists and exhibition of Indian films in Trinidad and Tobago, and by the nationals of Trinidad and Tobago coming to India to pursue courses in dance and music and as tourists. In the interregnum, India had also received the distinguished Trinidad-born writer/novelist Sir Vidia S. Naipaul. The exchange of visits of cricket teams of both regions has also assisted in the strengthening of bilateral relations. Incidentally, one of the better books written on cricket from a social scientific stand point has been by a Trinidadian, late C. L. R. James entitled *Beyond the Boundary*. It may be of interest to note that the first cricketeer of Indian origin to play for the West Indies team was from Trinidad, by name Sonny Ramadhin. Between the forties and the sixties, students from both countries pursuing their higher studies, have been interacting in the United Kingdom and in recent years in North America. In spite of these contacts, there exists a remarkable ignorance among a very large percentage of Indians about the very existence of Trinidad, its population, its resources and geographical location.

What does a small country like Trinidad with a literacy rate of over 90 per cent, want from India beyond the strengthening of its close historical and cultural relations? Put in another way, what does Trinidad have to offer that can be of benefit to a large country like India? These questions have greater significance in the context of a population of 1.2 million, a geographical area of 5,000 square kilometres, a flying time from Delhi to Port au Spain of about 17 hours and a time difference of 9 hours and 30 minutes GMT. The questions become even more relevant when one considers that trade between both countries is indeed very small, say in 1996

Trinidad imported a mere US $ 7 million in goods and services while exports were much lower approximating to US $ 2 million.

The major thrust of Trinidad's current relations with India is to increase trade between the two countries and bring to the attention of Indian entrepreneurs the excellent opportunities available for direct foreign investments, joint venture exercises and warehousing and storage facilities in Trinidad. Of course, historical ties will have to be strengthened, which could provide the necessary infrastructure on which new relationships based on trade and investments could be built.

Trinidad is keenly interested in having Indian tourists visit the twin-island state to savour not only its healthy climate and beautiful beaches but also its diverse cultural life style where churches, temples and mosques stand side-by-side, where festivals like Christmas, Easter, Diwali, Id, Phagwa (Holi) and Hosay are all celebrated by all sections of society regardless of their ethnic cultural background. The smallness of the society allows the visitors and the social scientists to see a practical and visible demonstration of this phenomenon of unity and diversity at every stage of their visit. There is no reason why Indian visitors to North America should not explore opportunities in Trinidad which would enable them to see something uniquely different but pleasant.

Trinidad and Tobago is a small and manageable state. In 1996, the rate of inflation was 3.4 per cent. Public sector foreign debt fell below US $ 1.8 billion in 1996 with debt-servicing dropping to 14 per cent of exports. As a consequence, the country has received high rating from the following two major international credit rating agencies—Moody's Investor's Services and Standard and Poor. Trinidad has the highest US foreign direct investment per capita in Latin America.

Trinidad has one of the most diversified and resource-rich economies in the Caribbean. The mainstay of the economy is oil and gas constituting 70 per cent of its exports, 27 per cent of its GDP and 24 per cent of revenue. Its major trading partner is the United States accounting for 45 per cent of exports and 35 per cent of imports. It is cultivating and expanding its base of export-oriented manufacturing industries. Trinidad is a significant producer of urea, direct reduced iron and asphalt. It is the only country where iron carbide is manufactured commercially and by the end of the century will be the leading world producer in the export of methanol and ammonium, as such Trinidad is considered to be the heartland of the Caribbean. In recognition of its natural, unspoilt beauty, its bountiful energy resources and its remarkable economic achievements, Trinidad is aptly referred to as "the Gem of the Caribbean".

It is noteworthy that over 50 American companies and a large number of British and other European companies are now well established in the islands. Between 1995 and 1998, US $ 3.5 billion would have been invested in Trinidad making it the most important US investment destination per capita in Latin America and the Caribbean. A significant proportion of this investment has already been realised in 1996 with the start of construction of a liquefied natural gas plant to the tune of US $ 1 billion in southern part of Trinidad involving AMOCO and Cabot (US companies), British Gas Company (UK), Respol (Spain), and Trinidad's own National Gas Company. The outstanding developments taking place in Trinidad's economy has led the US ambassador to Port au Spain to refer to it as an "unbelievable success story which is expected to continue".

Geographically located off the coast of Venezuela, Trinidad serves as the gateway to and bridge between the Americas. As such it constitutes a strategic platform for launching the economic penetration of rapidly expanding markets of South and Central America. Port au Spain is also the location of the headquarters of the recently established Association of Caribbean States (ACS). ACS consists of 25 countries which are washed by the Caribbean sea. It has a market of 200 million, a combined GDP of US $ 500 billion and a trade volume valued at US $ 180 billion. The siting of the ACS headquarters in Trinidad is another tangible manifestation of the respect and prestige that Trinidad enjoys among its hemispheric partners.

In a recent study published by the Federation of Indian Export Organisation (FIEO) entitled "An Export Strategy for India for 1996-2001", Indian exporters are urged to look seriously at Trinidad as one of the countries for the establishment of select regional manufacturing bases that would enable them to take advantage of the marketing arrangements it has both within and outside the region such as the Caribbean Common Market (CARICOM), the Caribbean Basin Initiative (CBI) with the United States, Caribbean-Canadian Agreement (CARIBCAN), Lome Agreement with the European Union and other trading arrangements with Latin American countries. Discussions are due to start between CARICOM countries and those of MERCOSUR for establishing trade relations between two regions. One major company with an Indian connection, Caribbean ISPAT, is not only firmly established in Trinidad but is increasing its investment with the steel industry. Officials of a major oil company and a chemical and fertiliser company from India are currently holding discussions with officials of Trinidad with a view to invest in Trinidad. Tata vehicles and Maruti cars are sold in Trinidad.

Indian entrepreneurs would find it refreshing news to learn that negotiations have commenced for the conclusion of a double taxation agreement and a bilateral investment treaty between Trinidad and India.

What then are the factors/elements that would motivate industrialists to invest in Trinidad? Investors would find in Trinidad the following—a well established, stable democratic system; political and economic stability and continuity; abundant supply of energy; strategic location; high literacy rate with English spoken and understood by everyone; highly skilled and trainable work force; long association with foreign investors and progressive, investor-friendly legislation; stable exchange rate with freely transferable currency; excellent advanced domestic and international telecommunications; good infrastructural facilities; sophisticated banking and insurance system; free zone area; and cultural affinity.

There is a wide range of incentives offered and extended through the "one-stop shop" investment facilitation department of the Tourism and Industrial Development Company of Trinidad and Tobago.

The areas open for investment in Trinidad and Tobago are: *(i)* agro-based and food-processing industries; *(ii)* projects related to natural gas; *(iii)* chemical industries downstream of the petrochemical and steel industries; *(iv)* textiles and garment manufacturing; *(v)* pharmaceuticals; *(vi)* aquaculture; *(vii)* computer and software; *(viii)* wood based industries; *(ix)* tourism and hotel development; *(x)* electronics; *(xi)* marine industries; *(xii)* offshore banking and financial services; and *(xiii)* information technology services.

Apart from being a member of several regional groupings, Trinidad is seeking membership into the North American Free Trade Association (NAFTA). Trinidad is of the view that it is eminently qualified for its membership in NAFTA because of its liberalisation and open trading policies. It is also participating actively in the process toward the formation of a Free Trade Area of the Americas (FTAA) which is expected to come into operation by the year 2005. The FTAA will create the largest free trade area in the world stretching from Canada in the North to Tierra del Fuego in the South with a market of more than 450 million people.

10

Prospects for India-Venezuela Economic Cooperation

—*Jocelyn H. King**

India is one of the largest emerging economies of today whereas the current accelerated growth of the Latin American countries are increasingly integrating with the global economy. Therefore, Latin America makes an ideal business partner for India.

The world has welcomed the revitalisation of the Venezuelan economy which in the past had undergone many difficulties. Since 1996 Venezuela is back on the track with the adoption of the so-called "Agenda Venezuela"—a set of economic policies designed within the stabilisation programme. Together with the steady increase of oil prices and net capital income accruing to Venezuela, it has contributed significantly to the economic recovery of the country. The stabilisation programme, among others included price control, liberalisation of foreign exchange and adoption of a social programme to compensate for the hardships of the society at large. At the same time, the pace of privatisation has advanced and the financial sector has been reorganised after the difficult experience of 1994. Figures show improvement in capital accumulation, balance of payments reaching a high of US $ 63 million, increase in the current account balance to the tune of 12 per cent of the GNP. The national reserves are over US $ 50,000 million and the public finances also show significant improvement with a surplus in public and central government sectors of 7.3 and 0.9 per cent of GDP. Given these fortuitous

* Jocelyn H. King is Ambassador of Venezuela to India.

developments the government has established a fund to finance the national debt thanks to which the country has been able to ensure micro-economic stabilisation. Also, by 1996 foreign direct investment had reached US $ 1600 million, thanks largely to the participation of foreign capital in the oil sector of Venezuela. The favourable financial balance has enabled Venezuela to meet its medium and long-term international commitments. However, imports decreased during 1996 due to contraction of consumption capacity but it is envisaged that in the current year of 1997 it will see some recovery. Presently, Venezuela is facing a major problem because of the high inflation, "a viral fever" and since the Venezuelans are not accustomed to the spiralling inflation, they are therefore very restless. However, during the last year, Venezuela saw a rise in wages in all sectors. Largely on account of the initiative taken by the government and an agreement reached with the trade unions, wages have been raised at around 25 per cent keeping in view the spiralling inflation.

Regarding recent initiatives in terms of forging relations with India, it may be said Venezuela is ready to be the best business partner of India. Indeed, Venezuela's trade figures are not encouraging, yet there are tremendous potentialities for cooperation in the energy sector because Venezuela is a major producer of energy. Although India is a large producer of oil, yet it is also a large consumer since 1994. Ever since Venezuela has been supplying fuel for power generation in India. Though it took a long time, it has been realised in 1996. It will be useful for Indian entrepreneurs to visit Venezuela and assess for themselves the progress that it has made in the power sector.

Venezuela will further develop its own technology and certainly would contribute for the power generation of India. Keeping in view this objective, in April 1997 a joint working group in the hydro-carbon sector was set up to explore and exploit other fields of collaboration. Admittedly, the solid presence of Venezuela in India can only be achieved through the energy sector which would certainly contribute enormously to bilateral trade as well as other activities such as investments in joint ventures. In the realm of trade India has good business possibilities with Venezuela in such product lines as pharmaceuticals, automobile parts, textiles and garments. Other areas of promise are mineral processing and software which can be advanced over time.

Already, there are instances of Indian entrepreneurs interested in Venezuela's privatisation efforts. In fact, a large Indian group of entrepreneurs in partnership with the Mexican company is participating in the privatisation in one of the largest steel plants of Venezuela. Needless to state, the business community entrepreneurs will have to be more aggressive. Indian industrialists should have to come to Venezuela and discover for themselves the possibilities for joint ventures. After all, it is the energetic enterprises of people such as Vasco da Gama and Christopher Columbus whose ventures made possible the Indian mango to become the national fruit of Venezuela just as the European potato became a popular dish in India

11

Economic Integration in Latin America with Special Reference to MERCOSUR

—*Elda B. Sampietro**

Principally, the South American Common Market (MERCOSUR) consists of four countries of South America—Argentina, Brazil, Uruguay and Paraguay. Subsequently, two other countries such as Chile and Colombia have been associated with it. MERCOSUR is not merely an economic area providing for trade exchanges among member countries. It is much more than that. In 1996, the primary members of MERCOSUR in association with Chile and Bolivia made a joint declaration on their commitment to democratic values and institutions. Towards the end of the same year the members made yet another declaration underlining their adherence to political dialogue and consultation. Besides, MERCOSUR has also evolved a legal core of conduct based on juridical principles. This was achieved through the Treaty of Asuncion and the protocols associated with it. MERCOSUR also provides for promotion of education and culture amongst the people of the member countries. Recent protocols have opened up possibilities for the students of the region to go for post-graduate studies in the different member countries.

In respect of the economic potential of MERCOSUR, mention may be made of the total gross domestic product (GDP) of the region which amounts to US $ 8 billion. The total area of MERCOSUR spreads over 12 million sq. kms. Without doubt MERCOSUR has contributed substantially to intra-region trade. Before the Treaty of Asuncion, intra-MERCOSUR

* Elda B. Sampietro is Ambassador of Argentina to India.

trade was valued at around US $ 4 billion. By 1996, on the basis of available data, it is estimated that intra-MERCOSUR trade has reached an amazing level of US $ 16.5 billion.

MERCOSUR is a regional set up offering immense opportunities not only for the private sector but also to the public and government sectors. Exports of three MERCOSUR member nations have grown from US $ 1.8 billion to nearly 8 billion in 1996. Equally, imports too have increased. In the beginning they were importing only about US $ 833 million whereas today, it has reached US $ 5.7 billion.

More than trade, MERCOSUR aims at economic integration of the region. Towards this objective, Argentina and Brazil signed a series of treaties and protocols beginning with the Declaration of Iguacu in 1985. In the following year, both Argentina and Brazil signed two more protocols which are called Acts—one providing for economic integration between the two countries and the other for promoting friendship, democracy and development in both countries. The protocols (24 in all) of these Acts relate to a number of issues including importantly tariff production and elimination of other non-tariff barriers. In 1996 again yet another Act signed in Buenos Aires paved the way for the establishment of a common market in the region.

Mention has been made of the Treaty of Asuncion which truly is an important juridical agreement signed by all the four—Argentina, Brazil, Paraguay and Uruguay—member countries of MERCOSUR. The main feature of the Treaty is the free movement of goods and productive factors and also coordination of the member countries' macro-economic and sectoral policies. Other commitments enshrined in the Treaty is to help organise our laws, norms and goals to help strengthen the MERCOSUR. The final objective of the Treaty is to promote development within the region with accent on social justice. All these entail that available resources within the region are put to proper and effective utilisation to conserve on environmental degradation, encourage physical integration and finally coordinate the micro-economic policies and effectively integrate the different sectors of the entire MERCOSUR economy. These efforts however, have to be gradual and spread over a period until some kind of an equilibrium is reached to make the economically integrated region of MERCOSUR viable and productive.

12

Recent Developments in the Association of Caribbean States

*—Usman Ali**

The formation of the most recent regional grouping in the Caribbean, Association of Caribbean States, known by the acronym, ACS, has been a natural consequence of the global trend of establishing larger regional groupings to enhance advantages of cooperation. The Caribbean comprises all the states, countries and territories washed by the Caribbean Sea. The Convention of the ACS recognises the importance of the Caribbean Sea which constitutes the common patrimony of the peoples of the Caribbean, and recalls the role the Sea has played in their history and as a unifying element in their development.

The Convention establishing the ACS was signed in Cartagena, Colombia on 24 July 1994. The ACS comprises 25 states. Its members include the members of the Caribbean Community (CARICOM), Colombia, Mexico, Venezuela, the Central American States, Cuba, the Dominican Republic, and Haiti. Dependencies of the British, French, Dutch and the United States in the region are eligible for Associate Status. The headquarters of ACS is located in Port au Spain, Trinidad and Tobago. The current and first Secretary-General is a national of Venezuela, Simon Molina Duarte.

While the ACS embraces a collectivity of countries with important common features, it also covers a broad diversity of national entities. The differences are clearly evidenced *inter*

* Usman Ali is the High Commissioner of Trinidad and Tobago to India.

alia by indicators of geography, demography, historico-cultural and linguistic backgrounds. In fact, it is the first time Spanish, French, Dutch and English speaking countries have been brought together in a regional grouping. Among the countries in the ACS are Cuba, El Salvador and Nicaragua which were excluded as beneficiary countries of the Caribbean Basin Initiative (CBI). The CBI was launched in 1984 to provide for duty-free entry for about 64 per cent of the sub-regional goods into the United States. In the ACS there also exists different agreements such as CARICOM, CACM, OECS, Group of Three (G3—Colombia, Mexico and Venezuela), Andean Pact, NAFTA and trade regimes (Lome Convention, CBI, GSP and CARIBCAN).

An interesting feature of ACS is that individual countries belonging to a particular group are also members of other groupings within and outside the region—Trinidad is in CARICOM and SELA, Colombia is in ALADI as well as signatory to the Amazon Cooperation Treaty and Mexico is in SELA, ALADI as well as in LAFTA.

The ACS comprises of about 200 million people, a combined GDP of some US $ 500 billion and an annual trade volume of US $ 180 billion.

It was at the Special Meeting of the Conference of Heads of Government of the Caribbean Community and the Common Market (CARICOM) held in October 1992 that CARICOM Heads of Government agreed to accept the recommendation of the West Indian Commission to initiate proposals for establishing an association of Caribbean states in order to advise both economic integration and functional cooperation. The Commission was headed by Shridath Ramphal, former secretary general of the British Commonwealth. The initiative for the establishment of the ACS has therefore come from the CARICOM states and was willingly welcomed by the other states in the region. CARICOM itself came into existence on 1 August 1973. Surinam became its fourteenth member on 29 June 1995. CARICOM was preceded by Caribbean Free Trade Association (CARIFTA) which was established in 1965.

At the historic, inaugural and path breaking summit held in Trinidad in August 1995, Heads of States and Governments of the ACS, conscious of their historical and cultural diversity and the separateness of their past, and yet of their proximity, adopted a Declaration of Principles and Plan of Action which emphasised commitment to the initiation of a new era in the Caribbean region, characterised by the strengthening of integration, consultation and concerted action in order to ensure greater cultural, economic, political, scientific, social and technological cooperation among peoples, governments and countries of the ACS. They further acknowledged that cooperation among the states, countries and territories of the ACS provided an ideal mechanism and a unique opportunity for responding to the challenges presented by the globalisation of the world economy, increased trade liberalisation and competition for investment and markets. Initial emphasis was placed in the Plan of Action on cooperation and concerted action in the areas of tourism, trade and transportation. It is felt that there is a great linkage between the fields of trade, transport and tourism. There is in fact a close synergy between trade and transport on the one hand, and between these two and tourism on the other.

With regard to tourism, ACS recognised the strategic importance of that industry and the need to develop a regional tourism strategy emphasising diversity and economies of scale as key aspects. The importance of environmental conservation was also stressed. Concomitant with this policy will be the measures to address issues of environmental sensitivity and national cultural heritage. The Heads of the ACS have also accepted the offer of Mexico to establish a regional programme for education, training and research in sustainable tourism.

Increased trade and investment is seen as providing new and enlarged markets and creating opportunities for the improvement of the region's competitiveness globally. The Heads have acknowledged the difficulties involved in harmonising the rules and disciplines of trade and services. In this regard, they have instructed the Secretariat of the ACS to execute a number of specific measures to ensure progress in areas such as trade liberalisation, trade and investment promotion and facilitation, inter-institutional cooperation and the overall follow up and implementation of the Plan of Action.

Critical to the promotion of intra-ACS trade is the recognition of the existence of unequal partners within the association and the need to adopt special measures to mitigate the adverse effects on the region and the sectors. Both within CARICOM and CACM, a clear differentiation exists between the more developed countries and the less developed ones, categories differentiated on the basis of both size and development levels.

As far as transportation is concerned, the Heads stress the importance of the principles of easy access and equal opportunity to affordable air and maritime transportation as indispensable factors in the economic integration of the ACS.

All ACS countries are in a state of transition. Global economic changes in trade and capital markets are making it imperative for countries to become more competitive in export markets. Preferential access is being eroded by the implementation of NAFTA, by the revised European Union's policies on bananas and by the successful completion of Uruguay Trade Round. The countries of the ACS which themselves already belong to one regional or sub regional group and have been undertaking economic liberalisation measures during the past ten years are fully cognisant of the need for accelerating integration and for developing closer linkages between countries, particularly in the areas of trade and investment as a means of boosting economic competitiveness. The ACS aims therefore at exploiting the opportunities presented by current international developments. In the case of CARICOM countries, it allows them to transcend the confines of its small community relationship and develop closer collaboration with a far wider range of neighbours.

As has been mentioned earlier, almost all ACS countries have participated in the initiative towards regionalisation and trade liberalisation. CARICOM, CACM and Group of Three countries have sought the removal of non-tariff barriers. In the case of the former two, there has been the establishment and subsequent reduction of common external tariff as part of the objective of creating a more open trade environment. They have also accelerated the search for new market opportunities by entering into bilateral and plurilateral trade agreements at the regional level. In addition, closer cooperation between Caribbean and Central American sub regions has taken the form of ministerial meetings and the establishment of a consultative forum for the analysis of opportunities for intra-regional trade and the exchange of information. The G3 countries have been negotiating closer ties with both sides of the Caribbean Basin including plans for a Mexico-Central American free trade agreement by the end of 1996 and Venezuela-CARICOM and Colombia-CARICOM treaties granting the Caribbean countries non-reciprocal trade access for 10 years.

Figures show that the United States is the most important market for merchandise exports from ACS countries as a whole. The European Union is the most important market for the OECS sub-group, given that production and export structures are heavily weighted towards bananas and sugar, for which the European Union is the sole market.

Some countries' exports like those of the Bahamas, Haiti, El Salvador, Guatemala, Honduras, Trinidad and Tobago, Venezuela and the Dominican Republic are primarily oriented towards North America. And will therefore be directly affected by both NAFTA and the Uruguay Round. Others like Barbados, Dominica, Guyana, St. Lucia and St. Vincent and Grenadines and Surinam rely more heavily on the European markets for their exports and may be shielded somewhat from NAFTA's trade displacement effect. These latter countries will be concerned with how the Uruguay Round affects market access in the EU. Since they now receive important European tariff preferences under the Lome Convention or GSP, their competitive position could worsen if there is major erosion of these preferences.

Intra-ACS trade, though growing, still represents a very small share of ACS overall trade. About 7.3 per cent of ACS merchandise exports goes to ACS countries. However, considerable variation exists in the share of these exchanges, as it ranges from less than 5 per cent in the case of Bahamas, Honduras, Surinam and Mexico to over 30 per cent in the case of Barbados, El Salvador, Grenada, Guatemala and Trinidad and Tobago.

Intra-CARICOM trade remains a small share of total trade. As a share of total imports, it amounted to 8.5 per cent in 1982, while the value of intra-group exports was 12.1 per cent of total imports in 1992. Among the major constraints facing the growth of intra-group trade are the remaining trade barriers and the absence of CARICOM trade payment mechanism.

Intra-Central American trade also has declined. Measured in terms of exports, CACM intra-group trade declined as a share of global trade from 26 per cent in 1970 to 13.6 per cent in 1992.

The speed and course of liberalisation differ from group to group as for instance in the case of countries of OECS. They face particular difficulties in liberalising their trade partly owing to their heavy dependence on customs revenue, which account for more than 50 per cent of all revenue in most cases, and their very limited export potentials.

Disparities in size and development levels complete the pursuit of free trade in the Americas. There is no greater evidence of this than in the recently formed ACS. While there can be no dispute today, even among the sceptics about the global benefit of trade liberalisation, the realisation of such benefits by small and less developed countries will greatly depend on their capacity to adjust to shifts in market opportunities and to increase competition. If they are unable to do so due to underlying structural weaknesses, their trade and economic prospects may worsen. This is clearly illustrated in the case of most ACS countries vis-à-vis the United States. Since the United States is the most active supplier of almost all goods which the ACS countries import, zero import duties to the United States would lead to direct and equal competition between domestic and US producers in the Caribbean Basin. Furthermore, unless the Caribbean countries were willing to forego all Lome Convention preferences, hemisphere free trade would also mean that trade barriers towards the EU would have to be removed. It is therefore in this context, granting temporary parity to NAFTA is vital to allow these countries to adjust to the demand of more reciprocal treatment. Until the time reciprocal trade agreements become an inescapable reality for ACS countries, several measures need to be implemented/continued *viz.* NAFTA-parity, continuing concessions from EU countries, deepening internal economic reforms and steady progress towards liberalisation and integration on the part of the Caribbean Basin countries.

The ACS need to increase intra-sub-regional trade to allow them to participate constructively in the drafting of hemispheric rules which expand or preserve market access without short-circuiting the World Trade Organisation. Greater cohesiveness among them would enable them to respond effectively to international economic changes.

The peoples of the ACS will therefore have to face the challenges and opportunities presented by the globalisation of the world economy, increased trade liberalisation and the need for cooperation in order to promote investment and wider markets in the region. They would have to prepare themselves to compete in a world where trade preferences are being eroded or, are in the process of being eliminated altogether.

The Heads of States and Governments have adopted the Plan of Action as a collection of integrating and closely relating measures to advance the development of the ACS region and committed the ACS membership to its timely and effective implementation.

13

Goa as a Nodal Point for India-Latin American Relations

—*Gopal Srinivasan**

Goa has one of the highest per capita incomes among all the states of India, which for the year 1994-95 was Rs. 17,881 and growing at an annual average rate of 4 per cent since 1980. The state's Gross Domestic Product for the year 1994-95 stands at Rs. 2243 crores with the share of agriculture being less than 15 per cent, manufacturing sector being 35 per cent to the GDP and the service or tertiary sector contributing 50 per cent to the GDP. Goa's human development indicators are even more impressive. Goa has a birth rate of 17 per thousand, death rate of 7 per thousand, and infant mortality rate of 17 per thousand. Since Goa's liberation in 1961, the emphasis has been on education and health care—Goa right now enjoys the second highest literacy rate in the country, *i.e.* 75 per cent. In addition, Goa has a high rate of bank deposits which in 1994-95 amounted to Rs. 3,728 crores with NRI deposits estimated at Rs. 1,233 crores. Goa is one state that generates one of the highest foreign exchange earnings per capita primarily on account of its exports, tourism and NRI remittances.

Goa Chamber of Commerce and Industry (GCCI) is one of the oldest chambers in the country established in 1908. For the last two years, the major thrust of GCCI is what we have designated as "Government and Business: Partners in Development". Keeping in view the new economic development, GCCI has initiated several dialogues with the

* Gopal Srinivasan is Executive President, Zuari Agrochemicals Ltd.

governments of Goa, Maharashtra, Gujarat and Madhya Pradesh in an effort to find and resolve solutions to many taxing problems. The Chamber also submitted a draft blueprint for the development of Goa, which among others, have sought for setting up financial institutions in the State, convention centre, privatisation of the infrastructures on competitive basis, delicencing etc. At the moment, GCCI's priority is setting up an offshore banking sector in Goa in keeping with the economic reforms and the needs of the industrial sector. Being a small homogenous state, Goa has its distinct advantages. It is situated close to Mumbai, the premier financial centre in the country. Efforts are afoot to establishing a software park in Goa with the state-of-art technology. Goa admittedly, can be an ideal place for an offshore banking centre, not only to cater to the needs of India but also possibly to the South Asian and other financial markets.

Confederation of Indian Industries (CII) is an apex industry association acting as a nodal point for Indian industries and the international business community. It has direct membership of over 3,400 companies with annual sales turnover estimated around US $ 63 billion. It has 23 offices in India and 10 overseas.

Latin America has long been considered as a "lost continent". It had a turbulent history of colonialism. After being subjected to years of military rule, changing governments and unchanging economies, order seems to have returned to the Latin American countries. Democracy has returned to this region and the Latin American countries today are busy further strengthening and consolidating the foundations of democratic institutions.

During the 1980s, Latin America suffered from low levels of average income and discouraging rates of economic growth. Whereas East Asian economies grew at an average of an impressive annual rate of 7.4 per cent, Latin America registered only 1.7 per cent growth. Since its population grew faster, the net result was that it slipped backward both absolutely and relatively. This vast continent has more than 400 million people in an area of almost 7 million square miles stretching from Rio Grande in the north and Antarctica in the south with a range of political cultures and socio-economic structures. Argentina's standard of living around 1900 suggested that it was a developed economy and very different from say Honduras or Guyana. Population change in Latin America occurs in distinct forms—countries such as Bolivia, Dominican Republic and Haiti have high fertility rates and lower life expectancy whereas middle group countries like Brazil, Colombia, Mexico, Venezuela, Costa Rica and Panama are beginning to experience decline in fertility rate and longer life expectancy; then the temperate zone countries of Argentina, Chile and Uruguay have demographic characteristics somewhat similar to the developed countries. Despite this diversity, there are reasons for considering the Latin American countries as an integral region for, one, the economic challenges confronting them are strikingly similar; two, these countries' domestic politics and processes, given their uniform fragility; and three, all of them being affected similarly by their relationship with the United States.

Several decades ago, Latin America's future appeared encouraging. Demand for its coffee, timber, beef, oil and minerals was high. Foreign investment was considerable in sectors such as agriculture, industry and infrastructure. Production of steel, output of electrical energy, metals and machinery grew phenomenally. Real GDP per capita rose at an annual average of 2.8 per cent during the 1960s and spurted to an annual average increase of 3.4 per cent in the 1970s. Unfortunately, between 1980-88, Latin America's real GDP per capita fell by an annual average of 2.9 per cent. Reasons for this reversal are very clear. Instead of encouraging industrialists to target foreign markets and stimulate the economy to export-led-growth like the East Asian NIEs, many Latin American governments pursued a policy of import substitution, creating their own steel, cement, paper, automobiles and electronic goods industries which were given protective tariffs, government subsidies and tax breaks to insulate them from international competition. As a result their products became less attractive abroad. Moreover, while it was relatively easy to create a basic iron and steel industry, it proved harder to establish hi-tech industries like computers, aerospace, machine tools and pharmaceuticals.

Secondly, economic growth was accompanied by lax financial policies with increasing reliance on external borrowings. Governments poured money into infrastructure and schools but also into state-owned enterprises, large bureaucracy and oversized armed forces paying them by printing and raising money for mainly US banks and international agencies. Inflation spiralled and became mind-boggling. For instance, in 1989 the rate of inflation had reached a dizzy height of 3400 per cent, Argentina 3700 per cent, Peru nearly 3000 per cent, Brazil almost 1500 per cent. Ecuador with 60 per cent inflation, perhaps is, the only country that did comparatively well. As a consequence, some among the Latin American countries found themselves among the most indebted countries in the world. Latin America's indebtedness around this time was estimated around US $ 1000 per capita. There was net capital outflow just around the very time when capital was critically needed to help facilitate economic growth. Starved of external capital resources together with the local currencies made worthless by hyperinflation, many countries of the region were placed in a serious economic bind than could have been imagined some three decades ago.

With the democratisation process beginning in 1980s civilian leaders had to face innumerable problems. One, related to the unimpressive accomplishment of the education system largely on account of neglect and under-investment in schools and colleges. Despite these setbacks, recovery began. Liberalisation and privatisation were set in motion. The opening up of the large Latin American market comprising over 500 million people offered attraction to foreign investors. Latin America is now ranked as one of the lucrative emerging markets of the world. In 1996, Brazil alone received US $ 13 billion in FDI and Chile more than US $ 4.3 million. Number of reasons account for these transformative changes of which the most important are the geographic and political proximity of the region to the United States and the richness of natural resources. It is estimated that over 15 per cent of the world's current resources are located around the fabled Amazon river.

Does India need Latin America, or does Latin America need India? Why is trade not increasing? The probable causes could be one, distance between the two regions; two, high transportation costs; and three, lack of information. There are four major trading blocs in Latin America—one, Grupo Andino consisting of Peru, Bolivia, Ecuador, Venezuela and Colombia; two CARICOM comprising all the Caribbean countries and Guyana; three, Group Three (G3) with Colombia, Mexico and Venezuela; and four, MERCOSUR with its constituent members in Brazil, Argentina, Paraguay and Uruguay.

MERCOSUR is ranked as the world's fourth largest integrated market after NAFTA, the European Union and Asia Pacific Economic Community (APEC). MERCOSUR has grown by an annual average of 35 per cent since 1990 and at US $ 5000 in per capita income.

Indo-Peruvian trade between January-September 1996 was US $ 43.5 million. India exports motorcycles, bicycles, tyres and tubes, three wheelers, pharmaceuticals, auto and bicycle parts, textiles and rice. Technology transfer has taken place in the manufacture of sponge iron. Bharat Heavy Electricals Limited (BHEL) has participated in a tender for making power transmission equipment. India would be interested in the rich mineral sector specially in the Bayovan phosphate project in northern Peru. Joint ventures and related economic cooperation can lead to more meaningful relations in the years ahead. However, there are some impediments such as one, absence of direct shipping links; two, infrequent visits of businessmen and business delegations; three, lack of participation in trade fairs; four, lack of direct air links to boost tourism and business; and five, the absence of a Spanish language website on India.

The president of the National Institute of Science and

Technology of Peru visited India last year to make a study of solar energy and use of genetic energy in agriculture as well as to learn about post harvest agricultural technologies, space programmes and research, satellite communication for making weather forecasts and assessment of natural resources.

Bilateral trade between India and Chile is estimated around US $ 125 million. Chile exports copper, timber and fish to India worth US $ 85 million. India exports mainly dyes, bicycles, hand tools, linen, rugs and leather, cotton, polyester fabrics and garments, chemicals and pharmaceuticals and also India-made Maruti cars. With its modernisation programme underway in sectors such as railways, mining and software together with its own rich oil resources in the southern pole and also being almost a corruption free state, Chile offers a band of opportunities for Indian entrepreneurs.

In Guyana too, opportunities exist for Indian companies. Kirloskar Group has already offered to buy the Guyana Electrical Corporation. Core Parental has recently entered the Guyanese market in activities such as welding electrodes, low cost housing, non-conventional energy generation, small-scale industries, rice research, mining and quality control of products.

Brazil's GDP is calculated at US $ 750 billion, almost 40 per cent of South America's GDP. Foreign investment was US $ 13 billion in 1996 with a foreign exchange reserves at US $ 50 million. Foreign equity participation is unrestricted. Areas where investments are mounting are transportation, electricity, telecommunications, ports, water distribution, sanitation, garbage collection, gas distribution and banking. Brazil is very rich in minerals. Its energy needs to some extent could be met by India with its technology to generate solar and bio-mass energy. Scope exists for Indian software exporters to get project and consultancy contact. Reciprocally, Brazil can supply agro-technology to Indian industries in sugar, alcohol, chemicals and food processing.

Over the years, many more possibilities for meaningful

economic exchanges can be identified between India and the countries of Latin America. What is therefore called for is to accelerate the process of the current pace of bilateral relations based on mutuality of interest.

14

India's Overtures towards Latin America and the Caribbean

*—Shailendra Kumar**

Rich in natural resources such as minerals, land and forests, the region of Latin America accounts for 5 per cent of world trade. Recent liberalisation policies adopted by most countries of Latin America has resulted in integrating the economies of these countries with the global economic system. Efforts at controlling spiralling inflation, reduction of external debt as well as tariff and non-tariff trade barriers together with economic restructuring and liberalisation of capital markets in these countries have greatly contributed to the positive development of the region. Today, the region is the second fast growing region in the world producing a variety of cash crops such as coffee, sugar cane, tobacco, cocoa, soybeans, grapes, maize, wheat, bananas and corn.

Recent regional integration arrangements like MERCOSUR and CARICOM have contributed to the collective strength of the region resulting in substantial flow of foreign direct investment to the region which is currently estimated around US $ 5 billion. Sectors that have attracted sizeable FDI inflows are automobile in Brazil and Mexico, and natural resources in Chile.

Before assessing what India should do towards Latin America and the Caribbean, it is necessary to know what other countries are doing in the region. Korea has in recent years set up a Latin America bureau in its ministry of foreign affairs

* Shailendra Kumar is Deputy Secretary, Ministry of Commerce, GOI.

dispatching joint public and private economic missions to Latin American countries to assess the potentials of Korean investment in such areas as automobiles, electronics, textiles, oil refining and agro-fishery industries for a targeted investment of about US $ 2.5 billion. The Exim Bank of Korea has extended a credit of US $ 150 million to the region. Following his visit to the region the president of Korea had stated that the region would be the new frontier for his country to explore. Today, Korea's trade with the region is around 6 per cent of the country's world trade. Of this, Korea's trade with Brazil alone is valued at US $ 3 billion as against India trade with the region which is presently estimated at US $ 600 million.

Next to Korea, Japan ranks as the second trade partner of Latin America in Asia. Following the exchange of visits by the heads of state of Japan and Brazil, the former has extended credit facilities to a host of countries of the region. Japan's trade with Brazil is currently reaching a US $ 5.5 billion figure whereas the total value of its trade with Chile is close to US $ 4 billion.

Unarguably, the United States both geographically and historically is linked to the Latin American region and has remained the largest trading partner. US-Brazil two-way trade, for instance, stands today at around US $ 19 billion. Also, the US is the largest investor in the region. The North American Free Trade Agreement (NAFTA), it is expected to enlarge beyond Mexico and encompass other countries of the region.

Next in importance in respect of investments is the European Union. Importantly, France and Germany are the two countries of the EU which have directed investment in specific hi-tech sectors including automobiles to countries such as Argentina and Brazil.

Against the background of the intense interest with which the industrially advanced countries of Europe, North America and Asia are forging relations with Latin America, the pertinent question that needs to be raised is why is India slow in its efforts towards seeking cooperation with the region. Without doubt India has an indistinct image in the Latin America-Caribbean region. Indian exporters consider Latin American countries to be too far from India and too insignificant in trade terms. Also, funds of our Indian exporters are blocked in various countries. Besides there has not been any serious efforts at a promotion nor a concerted policy for boosting trade with Latin America. India has for the first time participated in a trade fair held in Sao Paulo in November 1996. Also, India faces certain infrastructural constraints such as absence of direct air service to this region. Only now proposals are being considered to establish direct air service with some major metropolitan centres of Latin America. Again Indian commercial representatives are now present in the region to monitor business and trade opportunities. Only last year (April 1996), a consulate general office has been set up by India's Ministry of External Affairs. Neither does India have any direct shipping facility in the region. Since last year one shipping service from Bombay has been opened to connect Sao Paulo in Brazil. Efforts are also afoot to increase the frequency of the shipping service and enhance its speed (presently it takes as many as 22 days to reach Sao Paulo from Mumbai). Banking is yet another facility that Indian businessmen do not have access to Latin America. One representative of the State Bank of India is located in Sao Paulo.

On the basis of available data as of 1996, it may be possible to make an appraisal of the current trends in India's trade with Latin America. India's export growth has gone up by 50 per cent whereas the import is showing a negative –3.3 per cent. With Brazil, India's export has gone up by 55 per cent and with Chile 51.57 per cent. India has an export surplus with most Latin American countries. While India's trade with Cuba is insignificant, efforts are being made to revitalise it. With Mexico, India's export growth has reached 46 per cent in 1996 and Venezuela 30 per cent whereas with countries such as Panama, Paraguay and Uruguay it is showing negative trends.

Undoubtedly, to strike a trade balance and reduce the disparities in terms of the two-way trade between India and Latin America, efforts need to be made to institutionalise mechanisms that could correct the dispersions. It is with this objective in view, presently the Government of India is considering establishing joint bi-national business councils with at least for the time being twelve select Latin American countries. Also, efforts need to be made to institute a structured dialogue with some of the Latin American regional arrangements such as importantly the Rio Group and MERCOSUR. To this effect, the Government of India has already submitted a proposal to Brazil seeking India as a dialogue partner in MERCOSUR.

15

Summary of Proceedings and Final Recommendations

*—V. Shivkumar**

Divided into four sessions, the conference on "Emerging Trends in Indo-Latin American Relations in the 20th Century" was inaugurated by H.E. the Ambassador of Chile, Uldaricio Figueroa. Welcoming the delegates, Prof. V. Shivkumar, Director of the Centre for Latin American Studies of Goa University read the commendatory message of the Governor of Goa, H.E. P.C. Alexander and highlighted the focus and the significance of the conference. Chairing the inaugural session, the Vice-Chancellor of Goa University, Professor B.S. Sonde underlined the importance of the conference focussing on India-Latin America economic relations and stressed the need for an intense discussion on aspects of science and technology in forging meaningful relations. Delivering the keynote address, H.E. the Ambassador of Chile, Uladricio Figueroa spoke at length on the evolution of the Latin American countries and the significant contributions these countries have made on a number of initiatives such as in the realm of international law pertaining to peaceful settlement of disputes, human rights and liberalisation of world trade and so on. With the revitalisation of the democratic processes in Latin America and the rejuvenation of the economies of the region, Latin America, the Ambassador pointed out has regained the confidence of the international community. In his inaugural address, Shri Rakesh Kumar, Joint Secretary,

* V. Shivkumar is Director, Centre for Latin American Studies, Goa University.

Policy Planning Division of the Ministry of External Affairs, acknowledged that both India and the countries of Latin America have to discover each other in respect of the potentials they have for forging meaningful and purposive cooperation. In this effort he was of the view that the recent initiatives taken by both India and countries of Latin America would pave the way for accelerated bilateral relations.

The second session was chaired by Shri N. Krishnan, retired Additional Secretary of the Ministry of External Affairs in which the heads of Latin American and Caribbean missions made formal presentations. Each speaking about the countries they represented—Argentina, Brazil, Chile, Cuba, Panama (in absentia), Peru, Trinidad & Tobago and Venezuela—described at length the recent economic developments and the innovative policy measures which have been ushered in to integrate their countries in the global economy and also identified areas, economic sectors and opportunities that India could usefully harness for bilateral relations. Also, two of the Heads of Missions—Argentina and Trinidad and Tobago gave a graphic background to the economic integration processes in which their countries are presently engaged such as MERCOSUR and Association of Caribbean States (ACS).

In the third session devoted to a fruitful discussion on areas of cooperation in the field of science and technology, the scientists of Indian Space Research Organisation (ISRO) and the National Institute of Oceanography in their presentations narrated at length the specific expertise available in India in the field of science and technology. In the course of the discussion, the Latin American and Indian participants agreed that fruitful cooperative ventures can be undertaken by the leading research institutions in both India and Latin America on areas such as satellite communication, exploration of ocean resources, atomic energy, low cost housing, environment and ecology.

In the fourth and final session, chaired by General S.F. Rodrigues, Director, Goa International Centre, a wide spectrum of themes having bearing on aspects such as trade and commerce, joint ventures, science and technology collaboration and education and culture were discussed at length. The general consensus among the participants pointed to the immense potentialities that exist, which it was endorsed, have to be catalogued, carefully crafted into innovative policy measures and mechanisms by both India and Latin America and the efficacy to be closely monitored. In this connection, it was suggested that governmental agencies, business corporations and the Chambers of Commerce, academia and institutions of higher studies and research as well as the media would have to closely work together to make this endeavour possible and effective.

Shri S.P. Godrej, a leading industrialist and environmentalist of India, made the valedictory address. In the course of his presentation he highlighted the imperative need for building new and sustainable bridges with the Latin America-Caribbean region. It is high time he said, that the Indian trading and business community should overcome their obsession with the industrially advanced countries of Europe and North America and seek new avenues of cooperation with countries of the developing world importantly, Latin America.

Following were the recommendations that were formally made at the end of the conference.

1. In the area of trade and commerce, Indian business community should explore more intensely the Latin American and Caribbean markets and take advantage of the existing favourable relationship between the two regions. The principle of reciprocity should be enshrined in any bilateral trade agreement.
2. Adequate information should be made available to various agencies such as the Chambers of Commerce, trade centres, scientific establishments, area study centres by Latin American missions and the concerned ministries of the Government of India.
3. Government of India should coordinate with the Rio Group and the Organisation of American States and

should seek observer status and a dialogue partner in the other regional arrangements in Latin America.

4. At the level of the United Nations and other international fora, Indian permanent delegations should closely coordinate with their Latin American counterparts on major global issues.
5. Joint business councils should be set up with as many of the countries of the region to sort out pending problems relating to trade and investments and facilitate free flow of commerce.
6. Tourism promotion should be emphasised between India and Latin America which among others, could include not only vacation destinations but also cultural and religious centres of interest to people of both India and Latin America.
7. In the field of science and technology, scope for cooperation in frontier areas such as information technology, computer software, solar energy, marine bio-technology, satellite communication should be identified.
8. Exchange of technical personnel should be made possible to acquaint them with the technological developments in both regions.
9. Scientific and research institutions on both sides should undertake joint research programmes as well as for technical consultations.
10. Ministry of Human Resource Development and related autonomous bodies of research and studies such as Indian Council for Social Science Research, Indian Council for Historical Research, Council for Scientific and Industrial research, University Grants Commission and the Indian Council for Cultural Relations should adopt appropriate measures to promote exchange of knowledge and information between India and Latin America.
11. Cultural agreements between individual Latin

American countries and India should be reactivated so as to provide opportunities for joint/collaborative research and exchange of scholars and students.

12. Indian missions in Latin America should help disseminate knowledge about India both in terms of its history and modernisation through periodical seminars, conferences and other means.
13. Language expertise should be developed by the people in both the regions. Effort should be made to offer intensive training in Spanish and Portuguese languages for Indian business community, media persons and scholars and students. Efforts should also be made to offer courses on Indian culture and languages in some of the leading centres of higher studies in Latin America.
14. Efforts will have to be made to exchange media persons to help bridge the information gap that exists between India and Latin America.